The Ellan Vannin Story

The Ellan Vannin Story

Richard Stafford

Manx Heritage Foundation

Published by the Manx Heritage Foundation,
P O Box 1986, Douglas, Isle of Man IM99 1SR.
www.manxheritage.org

First published 1999
This edition 2009

ISBN 978-0-9562064-1-1

British Library Cataloguing in Publication Data
A catalogue record for this book is available from the British Library

Designed by Ruth Sutherland

Layout and typesetting by
The Manx Heritage Foundation

Printed and bound in Wales by Gomer Press Limited, Ceredigion

CONTENTS

to the 35
passengers and crew
who lost their lives when the *Ellan Vannin* sank
on 3rd December 1909

FOREWORD BY ROBERT QUAYLE

The loss of the Ellan Vannin may have occurred 100 years ago this year – but few people living in the Isle of Man are unaware of the event. Those who have passed through Island schools during the past 40 years will have learnt about it through the song written by Hughie Jones of the Spinners – and their parents will have heard it practiced and sung by those same children! Richard Stafford's work adds substance to the tale told in the song.

Although the loss of life was far lower, and the impact on the worlds' consciousness much less, to a small and closely knit community such as the Isle of Man, the tragedy was as traumatic as the much more infamous loss, three years later, of the Titanic. Ellan Vannin was far older than any tonnage a modern ferry operator would be allowed to deploy on an Irish sea route. But "L'il Daisy" was a reliable, trusted vessel, held in affection by crews & passengers and well regarded for her sea going qualities - and her loss remains a mystery to this day, notwithstanding the attempts to determine the cause of her demise at the time.

We will never know what disaster befell the Ellan Vannin on that stormy night of 3rd December 1909, but those who go down to the sea in ships recognize that, notwithstanding the relative robustness of modern vessels and the panoply of communication and navigation aids that make the task of modern day seafarers so much more predictable than their predecessors, the sea can still be an awesome place to be, and even in the calmest of weather, the unexpected can and still does happen.

The loss of the Ellan Vannin also activated a spontaneous but characteristic outpouring of generosity towards the bereaved families from the Manx community – both on the Island and from the Manx diasporate as well as amongst communities with strong links to the Island. The fact that the Disaster Fund was only wound up some 50 years later demonstrated the charitable nature of the Manx community and their commitment to support those amongst them whose lives had been touched by tragedy.

Much has changed in 100 years – but the Isle of Man Steam Packet Company still prospers in its 179th year and its vessels still pass, on a regular basis, the spot where the Ellan Vannin foundered. Never again will a vessel of the Company bear that name.

And Manx men and women today still recognize the power of the sea and sing with understanding that verse of the Manx Fishermens' Evening Hymn

'Thou Lord, dost rule the raging of the sea
When loud the storm and furious is the gale;
Strong is thine arm; our little barques are frail;
Send us thy help; remember Galilee.'

Ellan Vannin is remembered today with pride, affection and yet sadness, as are her crew and those passengers who lost their lives on that fateful night.

Robert Quayle,
Chairman,
Isle of Man Steam Packet Company.

THE SS ELLAN VANNIN SAILING INTO RAMSEY HARBOUR.

PREFACE

An old Eastern philosopher said that there are three things a man should do in his life: plant a tree, have a son and write a book. I have been fortunate enough to achieve the first two. The *Ellan Vannin*'s story has enabled me to complete the trio with an account of this very Manx ship.

The opportunity of researching the full history of the ship illustrates why the Isle of Man gives me so much pleasure. The interest of Manx people in their history and the ready offers of help and assistance that I have received are but two examples. I hope readers will get as much satisfaction in reading this book as I have had in writing it.

The story of the sinking of the Steam Packet's vessel *Ellan Vannin*, en route to Liverpool in 1909 is very much a story of the Isle of Man's *Titanic*.

However, there are many differences.

All of the *Ellan Vannin*'s passengers and crew were lost. Also, unlike the *Titanic*, the reasons for the sinking of the *Ellan Vannin* have remained shrouded in mystery.

This book is not just about the ship's final voyage to a watery grave. The history of the *Ellan Vannin* is charted, from its launch as the paddle steamer, *Mona's Isle*, through conversion to a twin screw steamer. There are descriptions of Ramsey, where the ship was based, as well as the passengers and crew on its final voyage.

There is a detailed account of the circumstances of the last voyage to try and answer the question of why the *Ellan Vannin* was lost. Much use has been made of previously unpublished material.

The mystery of the unknown female passenger is solved at last. The circumstances that caused a senior crew member to be suspended at the last moment and therefore miss sailing to his death will intrigue readers.

The book will appeal to those interested in Manx history as well as the shipping enthusiast. There is a full account of the Steam Packet at the time and the Company's part in helping the dependants of those lost.

Many people and sources have helped the author to compile this book. Mr Walter Gilbey, one of the Steam Packet's directors, suggested various people in the Company I should approach.

Shore-side I am grateful to Brian Johnson, the Technical Manager, and Geoff Corkish, the Communications Manager. On the sea-going side the late Captain Vernon Kinley, the Deputy Marine

Superintendent, advised on the practical aspects faced by the captain approaching the Bar in adverse weather. Captain Kinley's cousin, Geoffrey Kinley, is a barrister in London, with experience of Admiralty Law. I am grateful to him for his suggestions concerning the legal aspects of the Board of Trade enquiry.

Numerous other captains also advised on the nautical aspects of the ship's last voyage. I am particularly grateful to two former Steam Packet captains, Captains Bridson and Ronan. Tom Harrison, a Steam Packet officer, who has a particular interest in the history of the Company readily researched certain historical aspects of the ship. Alan Makin, a retired Steam Packet engineer, assisted with details of the ship's engines.

Captain Andrew Douglas has captained ships from the Isle of Man and his current position as editor of *Sea Breezes* provided not only the benefit of his practical experience of Irish Sea crossings but also some of the historical material in the magazine's library. John Curry, a Port of Liverpool pilot, advised on the hazards of the River Mersey.

I will always be in debt to all the staff of the Manx National Heritage library in Douglas for their unfailing support and advice. Particular thanks are due to Roger Sims, the librarian/archivist and Pat Griffiths and Alan Franklin for their assistance in accessing the Steam Packet's records in respect of the ship and the Fund established for the dependants of those lost.

Staff at the reference libraries in Southampton, Portsmouth and Merseyside Maritime Museum also rendered much assistance so far as the formal records concerning the ship and personnel. I am particularly grateful to Keith Hayward from Winchester reference library for his expert guidance on various sources of information.

The National Maritime Museum library at Greenwich was extremely generous with its ready offer of help and assistance as were the staff of the Guildhall Library in Aldermanbury which holds the Lloyd's Insurance Collection. Alan Giddings from Greenwich provided invaluable assistance.

There is limited information at the Public Record Office at Kew but a debt is owed to those staff who searched, in vain, for the Board of Trade file on the sinking.

Captain Brian McShane, the Marine Operations Manager of the Mersey Docks and Harbour Company, assisted me with the Harbour Board's

PREFACE

records concerning the sinking. So far as the weather was concerned I owe a particular debt of gratitude to Joyce Scoffield, now retired, from the Bidston Observatory on Merseyside. Ian MacGregor, the Met. Office archivist at Bracknell, also gave invaluable assistance as to the weather at the time the *Ellan Vannin* left Ramsey until she sank.

The *Ellan Vannin* was a mail ship. Artie Kewley from the Isle of Man Post Office assisted with trying to resolve the question of why the Island's mail went from Ramsey rather than Douglas. Two residents of Ramsey, Billy Corlett and Brian Daley, have great knowledge of Ramsey's shipping services and I am grateful for their advice on the shipping practices at the time and to Billy Corlett in particular for the loan of photographs.

The approach to Liverpool has changed from how it was in 1909 and my thanks go to Dave Clarke from the Hydrographic Office in Taunton who assisted me immensely with the description of the approach to Liverpool and also to Mike Gibbons of Winchester. Of constant support have been two gentlemen. My thanks go to Rory Addison, a lecturer in the Maritime Faculty at Southampton Institute and Jeremy Hyde, a senior officer in the Isle of Man Government. Martin Caley of the Economic Affairs Division of the Treasury assisted me with estimates of the current value of the fund established for the dependants of those lost. Advice on the nautical aspects of Ramsey harbour was readily given by officers from two shipping companies who use Ramsey - Mezeron Ltd. and the Ramsey Steamship Co. Ltd.

I made various appeals in magazines and newspapers and to others for information about the *Ellan Vannin*. To all of those who replied, (the number of responses I had make it impracticable to list all) I am extremely grateful. Without your response many parts of the book would not have been written. I would like to make special mention of John Curtis of Lloyd's of London, Mrs Bidmead from the Submarine Museum at Gosport near Portsmouth, my neighbours in Ramsey, Elizabeth and Fred Hodgson and Nick Corkill of Douglas Corporation, Frank Quayle of the Leece Museum in Peel, Ms Heather Osborn from Bordon in Hampshire, Chris Michael, the diver who has searched for what

remains of the wreckage of the *Ellan Vannin* and Pip Phillips from the Isle of Man Newspapers.

Michael Morris's drawing adds considerably to an appreciation of what the *Ellan Vannin* looked like. Ronald Evans of Pontefract has made a particular study of the ship's design. His plan and other material will be appreciated by the more technical reader. Dave Worth's assistance in advising me on the technical aspect of the layout of the ship was of great help. CPO David Hanscombe, currently serving with the Navy at Rosyth, has had a long interest in the Island's shipping and provided many valuable ideas for further research. Two general practitioners, Doctors Robin Harrod from Cheltenham and Jim Walton from Hayling Island assisted my research into certain of the medical aspects referred to in the book.

The Farmers' Combine in Ramsey was the largest cargo shipper on the *Ellan Vannin*'s last voyage. I am grateful to Mr J T Corrin of the firm for his assistance with tracing the record of how the Combine's claim, made against the Steam Packet Company for the loss of the cargo, was resolved.

Lastly, but by no means least, without the three people who typed the text and assisted with the wording there would be no book. I will always be grateful to my two sons Tom and Jon and to Wendy Randall. In respect of the text I had some assistance from a former literature teacher, Tony Benson.

Any book on a subject that ended in 1909 requires the assistance of many people. If anyone who assisted has been left out of the acknowledgments I extend my apologies. The *Ellan Vannin* sank on my late father's birthday. I have one passing regret: he did not live to see the publication of this book.

Richard Stafford,
Ramsey, October 1999.

Editor's note:
Since the first publication of this book in 1999, the author, Richard Stafford, has died. This new edition is published to commemorate the centenary of the loss of the *Ellan Vannin* and includes updated material in the Postscript.

ILLUSTRATIONS

CHAPTER ONE

RAMSEY AND THE ISLE OF MAN STEAM PACKET COMPANY

In the early hours of Friday, 3rd December 1909, the Isle of Man Steam Packet's ship SS *Ellan Vannin* set sail from Ramsey on one of her regular journeys to Liverpool, carrying cargo and passengers.

Although the weather was stormy when Captain Teare took the vessel out of the harbour, conditions appeared no worse than were frequently experienced on winter sailings across the Irish Sea. However, as the ship journeyed through the night the weather deteriorated. The following wind increased in strength until it reached storm force eleven - almost hurricane strength.

The *Ellan Vannin* managed to reach the entrance to the Mersey, but there, for reasons that have never been fully explained, she foundered. All fourteen passengers and twenty-one crew were lost. The vessel was later found submerged near to the Bar Lightship, broken in two with some of her plates staved in.

Subsequent events compounded the mystery of her sinking. One of her lifeboats was found floating on a nearby shore, and divers found that the davits on the *Ellan Vannin* had been swung out, giving the impression that there had been an attempt to launch the lifeboat. Yet the lifeboat still had its canvas cover on it, fully laced and untouched.

Some time later a message in a bottle was discovered on the shore at Hightown near Formby, north of the river. The message was apparently written by the cook of the *Ellan Vannin*, who claimed that the ship had been struck by another vessel and was sinking fast, but no other vessel was found to have been in a collision that night. Was the message a hoax? The cook's son insisted that it was his father's handwriting.

These and other events fuelled speculation on the Island and elsewhere as to the true nature of the events on that night, and to this day, the sinking of the *SS Ellan Vannin* has remained one of the most intriguing mysteries of the sea.

The *Ellan Vannin* had sailed from Ramsey, on the north east coast of the Isle of Man, which is set amidst unrivalled scenery at the foot of the majestic North Barrule, which rises to a height of 1,842ft and marks the end of the long line of rugged hills that march up the centre of the Island. Ramsey is surrounded by the fertile farmlands of the northern plain. The miles of safe, sandy beaches stretching from the cliffs of Maughold to the Point of Ayre are lapped by the waters of the Gulf Stream and add to Ramsey's appeal.

In 1909, as well as its attractions as a holiday resort, Ramsey had many advantages as a place for permanent residence. It had excellent communications by rail and sea, and weather conditions in Ramsey are said to be the best on the Island; frost being extremely rare.

The town is often known as Royal Ramsey, and this slight pretension dates back to the day in 1847 when Queen Victoria and Prince Albert visited the town. The royal couple were due to have landed at Douglas where the Island's leading dignitaries were waiting to greet them, but, because of bad weather, the royal yacht was diverted north to Ramsey. Prince Albert was struck by the attractive appearance of the town and its surrounding scenery and not wishing to miss the opportunity for a stroll, landed on the beach below Ballure Glen. Accompanied by various civic leaders, the Prince walked through the glen and on to Lhergy Frissel. During the Prince's progress a number of the town's citizens joined the party and the Prince freely entered into conversation with them. At the end of a stiff climb to the top of the hill at the south of the town, he was able to admire the panoramic views

'O Ellan Vannin, we are grieving sore,
Lost Ellan Vannin for the souls you bore
From that dark crossing to an unseen shore.

What was the story of that last farewell?
Nought but the ocean's voice remains to tell,
Tolling above them with its endless knell.'

'The Sorrowful Crossing' by Cushag

RAMSEY AND THE ISLE OF MAN STEAM PACKET COMPANY

THE AREA TO THE NORTH OF RAMSEY WHICH IS NOW THE MOORAGH PARK, C. 1870.

over the northern plain to the Point of Ayre, the vista stretching onwards to the Mull of Galloway, Burrow Head and the distant Scottish hills. To commemorate the Prince's visit a granite tower was erected at the spot where he stood to admire the views.

By the time the waiting dignitaries in Douglas were informed of the visit and had journeyed to Ramsey, the royal party had left!

Ramsey is the second largest town on the Island, and at the turn of the century it was served by two railways. The electric tram, which runs from Douglas up the east coast, still has its northern terminus in Ramsey. The steam railway ran from Douglas via St. John's along the less direct west coast route. The steam railway ceased passenger services in 1968, but in 1909 the track continued past the station and across Bowring Road running along the quay down as far as the Commercial Hotel at the corner of Market Square. There were sidings at intervals in order to provide direct rail access to the harbour.

Although the majority of shipping traffic to and from the Island used Douglas, Ramsey also had its share of business, and even in winter there were

regular sailings from the town. The services advertised direct from Ramsey to Liverpool in December 1909 were once a week, generally on a Friday. In addition to this there was a regular Packet service to Whitehaven on a Monday.

Like Douglas, Ramsey had a tidal harbour which meant it was impossible to berth vessels at low water. The opening of the Victoria Pier in 1873 solved the problem for Douglas, but it wasn't until the opening of the Queen's Pier in 1886 that Ramsey could cope with vessels at all states of the tide. Prior to this, vessels arriving at low tide had to anchor in the bay and wait, often after a long and stormy crossing, adding considerably to the passengers' discomfort.

The Queen's Pier was a magnificent construction, not least because it was some 2,160ft long. This huge length was necessary because of the gentle slope of Ramsey beach. In order for vessels to be able to get alongside at low tide, the pier had to go out into deep water. It was a popular place for a promenade, affording marvellous views of the town from nearly half a mile out in the bay, but because its main purpose was to facilitate passengers, it never had

RAMSEY AND THE ISLE OF MAN STEAM PACKET COMPANY

THE QUEEN'S PIER, RAMSEY.

the 'pleasure palaces' built on it like other notable piers on the south coast of England. Even so, an indication of the importance of the pier to the town is the fact that in 1906 it was used by 36,000 passengers.

For 84 years, up until 1970, the pier was a regular summer berth for Steam Packet vessels on the scheduled Douglas-Ardrossan and Douglas-Belfast routes, but as a result of decreasing numbers and the cost of servicing the berths, the pier was no longer used after the summer of 1970.

Ramsey has always been a thriving commercial centre as well as a market town. In the early years of the twentieth century it was a relatively large trading port, its principal export being agricultural produce from the farms of the northern plain, and some of the same businesses are still operating today.

The shipyard, now largely confined to carrying out repairs, was a thriving industry, building a large variety of ships the most famous of which was the *Euterpe* (renamed *Star of India*), which was 1,246 tons and 202ft long. Other businesses included fishing, a salt works, breweries, bottling of mineral water,

tanneries, smithies, a foundry and the growing retail trade, which was and still is largely centred in Parliament Street.

In 1909 the Steam Packet's agent in Ramsey was James Bell. His offices were in buildings on the East Quay, which are still called the Steam Packet Buildings. In more recent years the offices were occupied by Bevan Ltd, the electrical and marine electronic engineers. The Steam Packet motif can still be seen on the floor of the entrance hall.

In the summer season during the early years of the century the town was much frequented by families on holiday, and it was said that the society and mode of living were quite different to those experienced in Douglas. During the season the bathing facilities were excellent. On the north shore were the open air baths, and visitors were also offered the benefits of brine baths which were credited with curing many complaints. The brine was brought from the Point of Ayre salt lake through iron pipes, six and a half miles to the Ramsey Hydro.

Despite its charms though, some saw Ramsey as inferior to Douglas. In 1909 the Steam Packet's

RAMSEY AND THE ISLE OF MAN STEAM PACKET COMPANY

Tourist Excursion Guide said that 'the boarding and lodging houses in Ramsey are, on the whole, somewhat below those in Douglas', but the guide did concede that visitors to the town 'could enjoy golf at the Ramsey golf links.' To accommodate its visitors Ramsey used to have a large number of hotels and guest houses. With the decline in tourism in recent years, many of these have now closed.

In order to appreciate Ramsey as it was in the early years of the century, it is interesting to consider some of companies that made up the thriving commerce of the town.

The Mitre Hotel has long been used by visitors and locals alike. It has largely retained its exterior appearance and today it is mainly a public house and one of the few 'free houses' on the Island. Its main entrance is still in Parliament Street but with wonderful views over the harbour from the bar on the other side.

The Ramsey Hydropathic Establishment was also a thriving business. It is now the Grand Island Hotel which is about a mile from the town at the northern end of Mooragh Promenade. The hotel, which commands impressive views over Ramsey Bay, was originally a Georgian manor house. As a hotel it was much frequented by Victorian and Edwardian visitors, who came to benefit from its spa baths.

In 1881 the Town Commissioners had purchased a plot of sandy land called the Mooragh (meaning a 'void place cast up by the sea'). The Ramsey Town Act of 1865 had earlier authorised the buying up of the Mooragh for public purposes and the benefit of the town. The Commissioners were doubtless becoming conscious of Ramsey's growing attraction as a tourist area and with the pier and harbour improvements, the Mooragh would add to this attraction.

The construction of a bridge across the harbour was essential to the development of the Mooragh. One commentator of the time forecast that 'The Mooragh would be one of the grandest promenades in the Kingdom, being lined with houses and hotels second to none for the accommodation of visitors and distinguished residents.' The hotels and guest houses on Mooragh Promenade also added impetus to the need for a bridge.

The first proposals for a bridge were considered by the Commissioners in 1880, but the construction was considerably delayed and the bridge was not finally opened until 1892. The delay in building the bridge caused much of the early investment and interest in further development of the Mooragh to be lost, though this was further exacerbated by the collapse of Dumbell's Bank in 1900.

Although the Promenade was not finished as originally intended, the Mooragh Park was designed and developed and was officially opened on 11th August 1887 by the Lieutenant Governor, Spencer Walpole. A tablet in the promenade wall at the end of North Shore Road commemorates this event.

In the early years of the nineteenth century vessels sailed to and from the Isle of Man usually between Whitehaven or Liverpool and Douglas. This was the era of sailing boats and it was not until June 1815 that the first steamer, the *Henry Bell*, was sighted in Ramsey Bay. As the use of steam power increased there was an attempt to form a Manx company to operate a steam vessel in 1826, but after the purchase of a new steamer and a meeting to offer shares in her, the venture collapsed.

Residents and businessmen on the Island became increasingly dissatisfied with the services provided by vessels mainly run by the St. George Steam Packet Company (St. George Company). Graphic accounts of the harsh conditions endured by passengers fill many pages of Manx history. Passengers found there were no refreshments and limited accommodation under cover. A meeting was therefore held in Dixon & Steele's sale rooms in Douglas on 17th December 1829, presided over by James Quirk, High Bailiff of Douglas. The meeting was uncertain of the cost of a steam vessel but the sum of £4,500 was nevertheless subscribed. Further meetings followed and a company was set up and called the Mona's Isle Company.

The Company's first steamer was launched on 30th June 1830 at the yard of John Wood, Port

RAMSEY AND THE ISLE OF MAN STEAM PACKET COMPANY

Glasgow and named *Mona's Isle*. The *Mona's Isle* arrived in Douglas later that summer on 14th August and inaugurated the Douglas to Liverpool service two days later when she carried 15 saloon and 17 steerage passengers. The Mona's Isle Company provided a quicker and more comfortable crossing between Douglas and Liverpool than was provided by the rival St. George Company.

To compound their disadvantages, the St. George's best vessel broke up on the rocks in Douglas Bay in November 1830. William Hillary helped save the crew and was later instrumental in founding the Royal National Lifeboat Institution. The St. George Company shortly afterwards ceased to be a rival.

The Mona's Isle Company quickly established itself and on 11th July 1831 was awarded the important contract to carry mail to and from England. These mails had to be carried twice a week during the summer and once a week during the winter. A daily mail service was later introduced in 1879.

In January 1832 the Company changed its name to the Isle of Man United Steam Packet Company.

The word 'United' was later dropped. This company was the forerunner of the Steam Packet Company that we know today. So far as is known the Steam Packet is the world's oldest surviving company, operating regular passenger services, still trading under its original name.

Today the Douglas Harbour Linkspan agreement between the Steam Packet and the Isle of Man Government gives the company a monopoly on sailings. No such restrictions prevented nineteenth century entrepreneurs operating rival services. Having seen off the St. George Company, the Steam Packet faced another rival in 1836 which ran a vessel called the *Monarch*. Vicious price cutting followed but once again the Steam Packet emerged victorious, when the new company collapsed in 1837.

As the nineteenth century progressed the Steam Packet prospered. Ships were added to the fleet at regular intervals to help service the growing number of routes. There were to be services to Liverpool (at times two a day in each direction), Fleetwood, Llandudno, Whitehaven, Belfast, Dublin, Glasgow,

THE SWING BRIDGE AND HARBOUR, RAMSEY.

RAMSEY AND THE ISLE OF MAN STEAM PACKET COMPANY

Greenock and Ardrossan. Whilst Douglas was the main port on the Island, other Island ports were used. For example, by 1848 there was a direct Ramsey to Liverpool service.

The Isle of Man was starting to become a holiday island for those from Scotland and the north of England who could afford, what in the middle of the nineteenth century was a luxury, a holiday. By 1850 the Steam Packet carried nearly 50,000 passengers annually.

Nevertheless, the Steam Packet's domination of these routes continued to be threatened. For example, 1853 saw the establishment of the Ramsey (Isle of Man) Steam Packet Company the capital of which was raised mainly in Ramsey and the north of the Island. A new ship was ordered from Birkenhead. This was the *Manx Fairy*, a two oscillating engined iron steamer of 400 tons. As well as regular Liverpool sailings from Ramsey the ship visited many Island and Irish Sea ports on various excursions and carried a variety of cargoes. The *Manx Fairy* was not a financial success for its owners and after a few years and various mishaps it was sold. The Steam Packet had declined to purchase the vessel.

For clarification it should be mentioned that there had been another *Ellan Vannin* based in the Isle of Man which belonged to a rival company. This *Ellan Vannin* operated for a short period mainly from Castletown and sometimes from Douglas. She was an iron paddle steamer having a gross tonnage of 350 tons. She was built in 1854 but in 1858 she was bought by the Sardinian Government and renamed *Archimedes*. The Castletown company's *Ellan Vannin* was a short lived venture.

As an example of the comfort and style that could be enjoyed in a Steam Packet ship of the 1870s, the *King Orry* provided:

'a deck saloon with a white panelled ceiling with gilded mouldings. At the sides were mirrors and windows in a framework of birds-eye maple, divided by dark rosewood pilasters. The windows were fitted with silk curtains. The seats had velvet cushions. On the floor was a Brussels carpet'

The number of passengers carried by the Steam Packet continued to grow. By 1883 the number was approaching 300,000 annually. Again, rivals entered the fray.

One of the most serious was the colloquially named *Manx Line* which started operation in 1887. As had happened with previous competitors, there were races between them and the Steam Packet and some astonishing journey times were achieved. In the 1990s the Steam Packet's flag ship, the *King Orry* was scheduled to take four and a half hours between Douglas and Liverpool, but over a hundred years before, the *Manx Line* advertised a three and a half hour crossing! The *Manx Line* sold out to the Steam Packet in 1888 after price cutting made the venture uneconomical.

In the 1890s another rival, Mr Higginbottom, a Member of Parliament, twice tried to dent the Steam Packet's domination. Racing between rival vessels, cost cutting, and inducements to travel such as a free bottle of beer, were familiar features. However, as with previous rivals, Mr Higginbottom found the Steam Packet's fleet of eleven vessels along with the Company's experience and resources too much for him. He died in 1902 and his company was liquidated.

In the early years of the new century the Isle of Man was the playground of the north of England. Traffic increased. In 1903 the Steam Packet carried over 700,000 passengers. The directors of the Company were astute businessmen and the Steam Packet had thrived over 70 years. During this period the Company's reputation had grown. It renewed its vessels regularly with ships built to accommodate the Company's own specific requirements. The skill and experience of the captains and crew commanded respect. Innovations were readily accommodated; for instance in August 1903 the *Empress Queen* became the first Steam Packet vessel to be fitted with wireless.

The directors, as their minute book shows, took many of the operational decisions that today would be taken by the Company's management. The directors dealt with the hiring and firing and the terms of remunerating many of the employees. They were actively involved in appointing suppliers of goods to the Company and deciding terms. Perhaps this

RAMSEY AND THE ISLE OF MAN STEAM PACKET COMPANY

William Corkill
General Manager

Thomas Keig
Commodore of the Fleet

Charles John Blackburn
Superintendent Engineer

**MANAGEMENT PERSONNEL OF THE ISLE OF MAN STEAM PACKET COMPANY
DURING THE ELLAN VANNIN YEARS.**

attention to detail accounted for past successes and had laid the groundwork for the Company's continuing success in the twentieth century.

To conclude this necessarily brief scan of the Steam Packet's history it is appropriate to describe the main personnel, financial position and other events as we approach that fateful day in December 1909, when the *Ellan Vannin* sailed for the last time.

The General Manager of the Steam Packet Company in 1908 was Mr William Corkill, a position he held for twenty years. The Commodore of the fleet was Thomas Keig. He was appointed Commodore in 1907. The Superintendent Engineer, between 1895 and 1921, was Mr Charles John Blackburn. The Company's Liverpool agents since 1851 had been Thomas Orford & Sons (father, son, grandson and great-grandson), who operated from Drury Buildings, Water Street, Liverpool. This firm has now disappeared like much of the other commercial infrastructure at the heart of Liverpool, as the port has declined. The Company's newspaper correspondent (a paid-for appointment) was Mr T E Edwardes. Mr Edwardes edited those popular magazines *The Manxman* and *The Tourist*.

In 1909 the Steam Packet had the largest paid up share capital of any public limited company on the Island, amounting to £200,000. The next largest

company, the Isle of Man Railway Company, had a share capital of £190,000. Increasing expenditure or declining receipts might seem a relatively modern problem, but in *The Times* newspaper of 5th February 1909 the details of the Company's annual report were given. Receipts were £2,950 in excess of the previous year, while expenditure had increased by £5,091, but healthy reserves enabled a 6% dividend to be maintained.

In March 1909 the Company received a representative deputation on the question of improving steamer communications between Ramsey and England. Apparently during the 1908 season on Saturdays in August, the busiest month, the Company ceased to run certain services, causing inconvenience to English visitors. The Company decided to restore Saturday services and generally to increase steamer communications between Ramsey and England.

The question of Sunday services was always a contentious issue. As far back as 1831 there was a resolution preventing Sunday sailings. In 1908 it is reported that the Company conducted a poll of its shareholders to consider whether to operate a Sunday service. The issue appears to have been left to the directors to decide. In any event, the Steam Packet appears not to have run Sunday services during the *Ellan Vannin*'s time.

RAMSEY AND THE ISLE OF MAN STEAM PACKET COMPANY

Popular history maintains that the sinking of the *Ellan Vannin* was the only time that a Steam Packet ship has been lost in peacetime. It is also claimed that that in the 79 years before the sinking of the *Ellan Vannin* the Steam Packet had never lost a passenger's life. Sadly, neither of these assertions is true.

The first loss to recall is that of the *Mona II*. The *Mona II* had a gross tonnage of 562 tons and was an iron single screw steamer which had been launched in 1878. On 5th August 1883, whilst she was at anchor in dense fog in the Formby Channel near the Mersey Bar Lightship, the Spanish steamer *Rita* ran into her. The *Mona* sank in approximately 30 minutes although all her crew and two lady passengers were picked up by the tug *Conqueror*.

The next loss was of the *Peveril*. She had a gross tonnage of 561 tons and was a steel twin screw steamer. She was launched in 1884. She sank 12 miles from Douglas en route from Liverpool in the early hours of the morning of 17th September 1899 after a collision with the *Monarch* which was on a passage from Workington to Cardiff. Although it was clear that both the *Monarch* and the *Peveril* were on a collision bearing, neither altered course and the

Monarch struck the *Peveril* amidships on the starboard side. The engine room was flooded and the *Peveril* sank within approximately 40 minutes. Her crew and one passenger were transferred to the *Monarch* and later landed at Douglas.

It was fortunate for the Company that the sinkings did not cause a loss of life, and this was mainly due to the other vessels involved remaining in the vicinity after the collisions to render assistance. But lives were lost on the Company's vessel the *Fenella* in January 1899 when three passengers, who refused to go below, were washed from the decks in heavy seas.

As we shall see later, one of the earliest explanations for the loss of the *Ellan Vannin* was that the vessel had sunk after a collision with another ship. Certainly collisions in the Mersey involving the Company's vessels were not unknown. The *Douglas III* had a gross tonnage of 774 tons and was a single screw steamer. She was launched in 1899 for the London & South Western Railway Company and was acquired by the Steam Packet in 1901 to replace the sunken *Peveril*. In November 1903 she collided with and sank the *City of Lisbon* in the Mersey.

Twenty years later the roles were reversed. On

LANDING STAGE. LIVERPOOL.

LIVERPOOL'S FAMOUS FLOATING DOCK.
ON HER FATEFUL VOYAGE THE ELLAN VANNIN WAS HEADING FOR SALISBURY DOCK.

RAMSEY AND THE ISLE OF MAN STEAM PACKET COMPANY

16th August 1923 the *Douglas III* had pulled away from Brunswick Dock in Liverpool bound for Douglas. She tried to cross the path of another ship. However the Douglas collided with the 5,731 ton *Artemisia* inward bound from Java with a cargo of sugar. The Douglas sank but fortunately all the crew and 15 passengers were taken off safely. After lengthy proceedings through the Admiralty Court and the Court of Appeal, the House of Lords found that the *Douglas* was solely responsible for the collision.

Records are not as detailed in respect of the very early vessels as compared with later vessels. It was not necessary to survey and register shipping in the Isle of Man until 1885. The Court of Tynwald passed an Act in that year requiring passenger ships used on the coasts of the Island to be surveyed.

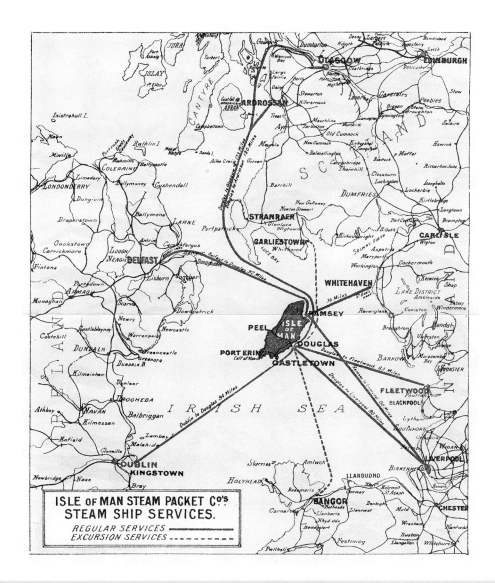

THIS 1909 MAP SHOWS THE PORTS SERVED BY THE STEAM PACKET.

AN EARLY STEAM PACKET POSTER DATING FROM ABOUT 1890. THE PADDLE STEAMER DEPICTED IS THOUGHT TO BE ONE THAT WAS BOUGHT FROM THE RIVAL MANX LINE WHICH SOLD OUT TO THE STEAM PACKET IN 1888.

CHAPTER TWO

THE SS ELLAN VANNIN

MONA'S ISLE II AT GLASGOW.

The *S S Ellan Vannin* started life as *Mona's Isle II*. Her predecessor, *Mona's Isle (I)* was in fact the first of the Company's vessels. She was a 200 ton wooden paddle steamer and she inaugurated the service that became the backbone of the Company: Douglas to Liverpool. Whilst the vessel was sold for breaking up in 1851, her bell is now preserved in the Manx Museum in Douglas.

'Then memories sweet and tender
Come like music's plaintive flow
Of the hearts in Ellan Vannin
That loved me long ago;
And I give with tears and blessings
My fondest thoughts to thee,
My own dear Ellan Vannin
And all those lost at sea'

The Manx song 'Ellan Vannin' with amendments

Mona's Isle II was built as an iron paddle steamer by Tod & McGregor, Meadowside, Glasgow. As well as working for the Steam Packet, Tod & McGregor established a reputation for building passenger liners for such well known owners as Cunard, the Inman Line and P & O. After many changes, what remained of the business was finally closed by Harland & Wolff Ltd in 1962. *Mona's Isle II* was launched on 10th April 1860 and had a raked stem, two masts and a single funnel abaft on the stern side of the paddles. She was the Company's ninth vessel. Her official number was 27260 and she had PQMG as her signal letters. Her measurements were: length - 200 feet, 6 inches; breadth - 22 feet, 2 inches and draught - 10 feet, 7 inches. Her maximum speed was 12 knots and she was reported to have a gross tonnage of 339 tons. The cost of production was £10,673. (Further technical details are given in Appendix I).

Camparison with the previous three vessels ordered by the Steam Packet, shows that the *Mona's Isle*

THE SS ELLAN VANNIN

II was by no means the fastest vessel the Company had. The *Tynwald*, launched in 1846, had a maximum speed of 14 knots and a gross tonnage of 700 tons; the *Mona's Queen*, launched in 1852, had a maximum speed of 13 knots and a gross tonnage of 600 tons; and the vessel immediately prior to *Mona's Isle II* was the *Douglas* which was launched in 1858 and was also an iron paddle steamer. She cost £22,500, had a gross tonnage of 700 tons, and was capable of 17 knots. In comparison with these vessels the *Ellan Vannin* was slower, although not much slower than the *Tynwald* and *Mona's Queen*, but smaller than all three vessels.

Mona's Isle II joined the fleet in June 1860. She was later described by the wife of a former Lieutenant Governor of the Island, the Dowager Lady Loch, as being well known during the nineteen years her Ladyship spent at Government House as a 'good sea boat'.

During her years at sea the *Mona's Isle II* had her share of casualties and similar incidents:

On 29th November 1872 she was in a collision with the *Agnes* near Ramsey. The *Agnes* was a schooner en route from the Clyde to her home port of Fleetwood. Despite the damage to both vessels they were able to put into Ramsey.

On 5th February 1873 she was carrying a general cargo and went ashore in fog at Ashton near Gourock on the Clyde. She was refloated later the same day at highwater and proceeded to Glasgow.

On 14th December 1878 she was grounded in dense fog on the Burbo Bank at the mouth of the River Mersey en route to Liverpool. The mail she was carrying was landed at New Brighton by boat. She suffered no damage.

On 13th December 1879 the steamer *Holly* was damaged near Greenock when she fouled the anchor of the *Mona's Isle II*. The *Holly* had to return to Glasgow for repairs.

None of these incidents was too serious and in 1882 the hull of the *Mona's Isle II* was considered sound enough to warrant her conversion to a twin screw steamer with a straight stem. The conversion took place at Westray, Copeland & Co, Barrow-in-Furness, a firm which did similar work on some of the Company's other vessels. In May of 1882 the Steam Packet launched a new 1,564 ton paddle steamer and named her the *Mona's Isle III*. The *Mona's Isle II*, now refitted, was renamed the *Ellan Vannin* in November 1883.

Following conversion the *Ellan Vannin* had a slightly shorter length of 198 feet, 6 inches. The breadth and draught remained the same. The *Ellan Vannin* had a slightly increased speed of 13 knots compared with the 12 knots as *Mona's Isle II*.

Unlike many of the Steam Packet's other vessels there were no shares in the *Ellan Vannin* that were mortgaged. The *Ellan Vannin* retained the official number and signal letters of *Mona's Isle II*. For completeness it should be added that registration remained at Douglas.

In the quarter century that the *Ellan Vannin* voyaged through the Irish Sea she acquired that 'old pair of slippers feeling.' She was relatively old, small and slow. The description of the *Ellan Vannin* in a letter to the *Shipping Telegraph* in 1898 was understandable. She was perhaps, as the correspondent suggested 'an antiquated specimen of naval architecture which ought to have been alongside Nelson's battleships'. Nevertheless, like that 'old pair of slippers', the *Ellan Vannin* generated affection. Many residents, so it is said, named their houses *Ellan Vannin* because of the regard and esteem in which the ship was held. Indeed, such was the *Ellan Vannin*'s loyal service to the Company year after year that in later years she was looked on as the mascot of the fleet and known by Manx sailors as '*Li'l Daisy*'. Manx sailors often said of the *Ellan Vannin* that she was the safest vessel afloat. She was a veritable *Ben-my-Chree*, a girl of a sailor's heart, and no finer vessel of her size was ever built.

Feelings about the Ellan Vannin generated the following ditty in the Ramsey Courier and Northern Advertiser of 14th March 1899:

'She's an antiquated ship with an antiquated crew,
She makes antiquated passages all the year through.
Between herself and Maughold Head there has been many a test
Of which the 'Daisy' has however always slightly had the best'

THE SS ELLAN VANNIN

Certainly stormy weather was no deterrent to her. It has been told that when a score or more of ocean steamers had been taking shelter in Ramsey Bay, the little *Ellan Vannin* had threaded a way through them, steamed to Whitehaven and returned in the evening, the completion of her voyage being heralded by the craft in the bay, still waiting for better weather, sounding their whistles. But that life aboard the *Ellan Vannin* could be hard is illustrated by a bad weather incident in March 1898. The *Ellan Vannin* had no steam powered steering mechanism and was steered by hand. The weather was so rough that in order to enter Ramsey harbour four of the crew had to manoeuvre the steering wheel against the force of the wind and sea.

In many respects the story of the *Ellan Vannin* reflected the story of life on the Isle of Man at the end of the nineteenth century. In March 1898, for example, she brought 80 navvies from Glasgow to Ramsey to work on the extension of the electric railway from Laxey to Ramsey. Another trip from Glasgow to Ramsey early in 1902 brought the first swans to Mooragh Park where their descendants can be seen today. The swans were gifted by Queen Victoria.

But in September 1900 there was fear that less welcome guests might be brought in from Glasgow. The Scottish city was suffering from a bubonic plague which caused 16 deaths. Rats, it was thought, could spread this plague to Ramsey. When the *Ellan Vannin* arrived from Glasgow she was effectively quarantined. She did enter the harbour but was anchored and secured at the harbour entrance. To prevent the vermin getting ashore, cone shaped discs were put on the mooring ropes. The breakwater was also fenced off and a guard was stationed with a dog to catch any rats that might somehow get ashore.

In his book *The Isle of Man Steam Packet Co. Limited 1830-1904*, A W Moore, a former speaker of the House of Keys described the *Ellan Vannin* as:

'One of the most remarkable and probably one of the most profitable boats in the Company's history, and still doing good work'. It was later said by the Steam Packet's General Manager that the *Ellan Vannin* made £2,000 per year for the Company.

The reason for these tributes can easily be seen when one looks at the *Ellan Vannin*'s vigorous sailing schedule. In 1901, for example, it was:

Monday:
Ramsey to Whitehaven.
Whitehaven to Ramsey.
Ramsey to Douglas.

Tuesday:
Douglas to Glasgow.

Wednesday:
Glasgow to Douglas.
Douglas to Liverpool.

Thursday:
Liverpool to Douglas.
Douglas to Ramsey.

Friday:
Ramsey to Liverpool.

Saturday:
Liverpool to Ramsey.
Ramsey to Douglas.

Sunday:
In port at Douglas.

Monday:
Douglas to Belfast.
Belfast to Douglas.
From Tuesday the cycle continues as before.

However, in the stormy Irish Sea as well as in more sheltered waters, the *Ellan Vannin* had her share of accidents. For example, close to what became her home port, Ramsey, is the Bahama Bank which lies about six miles away. The Bank is said to be named after an eighteenth century sailing ship, the *Bahama*, which met her end there. This hazard to vessels approaching Ramsey from the north used to be indicated by a lightship which was removed in 1915 when Maughold lighthouse came on stream. However, in July 1891, the *Ellan Vannin* was making for Ramsey when she came into contact with the watch buoy at the south of the Bank. The Captain was conscious that the speed of the vessel had dropped but was not certain why until the *Ellan Vannin* arrived in Ramsey harbour. It was discovered that the chain and iron weight used to anchor the buoy had been towed into harbour fouling the *Ellan Vannin*'s propeller. The buoy itself had apparently broken adrift.

THE SS ELLAN VANNIN

Indeed throughout her career the *Ellan Vannin* suffered a series of minor mishaps too numerous to mention here. However on the Clyde on 6th February 1900 en route to Glasgow she was quite badly damaged; she was in collision with the Anchor Line's steamer, *Astoria*. A portion of the *Ellan Vannin*'s bridge, as well as a lifeboat, were carried away. The deck was holed but she did not leak. Meanwhile the *Astoria* proceeded to New York undamaged. Whilst repairs were carried out the Ramsey-Liverpool service for passengers was suspended. Arrangements were made for passengers to travel free by train or electric tram to Douglas to connect with Douglas sailings to Liverpool. The Steam Packet chartered the *Sarah Blanche* to assist with Ramsey cargo carryings. The repairs were carried out by A & J Inglis, of Patrick, Glasgow, at a cost of about £800.

The *Ellan Vannin* had previously been involved in another collision on the Clyde on 28th December 1892. She collided with the steamer *Hare* from Londonderry. Both ships were considerably damaged.

Lest it be thought that the *Ellan Vannin* was always the vessel in trouble, three incidents where she assisted other vessels should be mentioned. Firstly in October 1885 the Norwegian brig *Professo* dragged her anchor in Ramsey Bay. The Captain and a Ramsey pilot were taken off by the lifeboat. The *Ellan Vannin* towed the *Professo* into harbour. Secondly in October 1886 the *Ellan Vannin* offered assistance to the *Vulcan*, which was carrying coal from Whitehaven to Douglas. Although the lifeboat stood by because of the *Vulcan*'s difficulties and the *Ellan Vannin* offered assistance, the *Vulcan* was able to proceed on its own. On another occasion the *Ellan Vannin* attempted to tow the Midland Railway Company's steamer *Donegal* off the beach at the Point of Ayre, the northern-most tip of the Isle of Man.

During the nearly 50 years of her life as both the *Mona's Isle II* and as the *Ellan Vannin*, the vessel underwent many changes and overhauls. One of the most important of these was the 1891 special overhaul at the Naval Armament and Construction works in

THE ELLAN VANNIN MAKING GOOD PROGRESS IN SLIGHTLY CHOPPY SEAS.

THE ELLAN VANNIN STORY

THE SS ELLAN VANNIN

THE ELLAN VANNIN IN DOUGLAS HARBOUR WITH THE STEAM PACKET'S HEADQUARTERS, IMPERIAL BUILDINGS, TO THE RIGHT.

Barrow, which cost £2,914. However there were various others. Some alterations were too minor to have merited recording and even the details of the more major changes have not survived. For example at some stage a new main deck costing £5,000 was fitted.

The insurers' requirements ensured that the Steam Packet's vessels received regular inspections and surveys. These could have been undertaken either by Lloyd's or the Board of Trade. Many Lloyd's surveys and reports have survived. However, the Steam Packet used the Board of Trade and their records have not generally been kept.

Despite such adverse comments as 'she's had so many repairs that the only thing that's old about the *Ellan Vannin* is her name', the *Ellan Vannin* received an annual No 1 Board of Trade certificate on 16 September 1909. This meant that the *Ellan Vannin* could carry 106 first class passengers on deck and 28 in cabins and 140 third-class passengers on deck and 25 in cabins. The total passenger capacity was 299. The minimum crew number was 14. From a practical point of view in her final days, it is doubtful if she ever reached anywhere near carrying her maximum load of passengers. What were carried in hundreds though,

were sheep. For example, on 28th October 1893 the *Ramsey Courier and Northern Advertiser* newspaper reported that the *Ellan Vannin* had landed about 800 sheep at Ramsey from Glasgow. On 1st November 1894 the *Ellan Vannin* landed 400 sheep at Ramsey from Ardrossan. In addition to sheep, horses, cattle, pigs and other stock were also frequently carried.

Indeed by the time of what was to be her final year, 1909, the *Ellan Vannin* was principally a cargo ship sailing to Liverpool, Whitehaven and Glasgow from Douglas and Ramsey, though she had also been for some years the regular passenger steamer on the Liverpool to Ramsey run which was direct during the winter season. She left Ramsey on a Friday morning and returned from Liverpool on a Saturday. Towards the end of her career she sailed from Ramsey, and by 1909 she was the oldest mail steamer in the world.

In 1909 the Steam Packet fleet comprised thirteen ships, nine with electric light, the biggest of which was the 2,651 ton *Ben-my-Chree III*. The *Ellan Vannin* had not been electrified and was still lit by oil lamps which would have been fitted in gimbals designed to keep the lamp vertical whatever the angle of the ship. She was the smallest and slowest vessel in

the fleet and understandably she was not listed as one of the Company's principal passenger ships.

After she sank there were rumours that it had been intended to take the *Ellan Vannin* out of service when she reached her half century on 10th April 1910. However, she sank four months before reaching this milestone. There is no evidence that the Company intended to run her for only another four months. Whilst her days were numbered it is reasonable to assume she would have lasted another summer season when traffic was at its busiest. Perhaps the autumn of 1910 would have seen the last sailing of the *Ellan Vannin*, but, as events unfolded, not only did she not see another summer, she did not even see her half century.

THE ELLAN VANNIN PASSING THE RED PIER AS SHE LEAVES DOUGLAS HARBOUR.

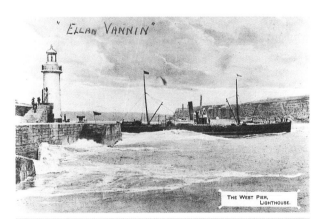

THE ELLAN VANNIN AT THE ENTRANCE TO WHITEHAVEN HARBOUR.

No. 3666.   Registered as a Newspaper

SAILINGS.

Isle of Man Steam Packet Co.Ltd
:o:
DECEMBER SAILINGS.
—:o:—
LIVERPOOL AND DOUGLAS.

From DOUGLAS. — Weekdays, 9 a.m., except 25th and 27th, 1 a.m. Extras: 24th 4 p.m.; 28th, 1 a.m.

From LIVERPOOL.—Weekdays, 11-30 a.m. (except 24th, 10-30 a.m.) Extras: 24th, 4 p.m. and 12-50 midnight.

CHRISTMAS HOLIDAY SAILINGS.

From DOUGLAS.—23rd, 9 a.m.; 24th, 9 a.m. and 4 p.m.; 25th and 27th, 9 a.m.; 28th, 1 a.m. and 9 a.m.; 29th to 31st, 9 a.m.

From LIVEROOL.—23rd, 11-30 a.m.; 24th, 10-30 a.m., 4 p.m., and 12-50 night; 25th and weekdays to 31st, 11-30.

LIVERPOOL AND RAMSEY.

From RAMSEY.—(Direct) Fridays 3rd, 1 a.m.; 10th, 9 a.m.; 17th and 31st, 1 a.m.; Thursday, 23rd, 9 night.

From LIVERPOOL.—(Direct) Saturdays 4th, 9 a.m.; 11th, 11 a.m.; 18th, 8 a.m.; Friday, 24th, 10 night.

BELFAST AND DOUGLAS.
(Calling at Ramsey.)

From DOUGLAS (Greenwich time.)— Monday, 27th, 11 night.

From BELFAST (Irish time.)—Tuesday, 28th, 12 noon.

GLASGOW AND DOUGLAS.
(Calling at Ramsey.)

From DOUGLAS to GLASGOW and GREENOCK.—Tuesday 7th, 6 a.m.; Monday 20th, 6 night.

From GLASGOW.—Wednesday, 8th, 9 a.m.; Tuesday 21st, 7 p.m.; and from GREENOCK on arrival of trains leaving Glasgow—Central at 10-10 a.m. on 8th; 9 p.m. on 21st; St. Enoch at 10-5 a.m. on 8th, 9-30 p.m. on 21st.

WHITEHAVEN AND RAMSEY.

From RAMSEY.—Monday 13th, 9 a.m.

From WHITEHAVEN (with cargo for Douglas)—Monday 13th, 9-30 p.m.

Passengers, their Luggage, Live Stock, and Goods, conveyed subject only to the conditions of carriage of the Company, as exhibited in their Offices and on board their steamers

Messrs ORFORD and Son, Liverpool
Wm. M. CORKILL, Sec. and Manager

THE RAMSEY COURIER AND NORTHERN ADVERTISER OF TUESDAY NOVEMBER 30TH, 1909, SHOWS THE STEAM PACKET'S DECEMBER SAILINGS. WHAT WAS TO BE THE ELLAN VANNIN'S LAST IS SHOWN UNDER LIVERPOOL AND RAMSEY (DIRECT) FRIDAY 3RD, 1AM.

CHAPTER THREE

THE JOURNEY

The S S *Ellan Vannin* had arrived at Ramsey harbour from Douglas on Thursday 2nd December 1909 and her discharge and loading started at 3pm finishing by 7pm. In addition to the crew twenty-five men were involved in these activities at a cost of £2 9s 9d. She was due to sail to Liverpool six hours later at 1.00am on the Friday morning, just two hours before high tide.

Just over 60 tons of cargo were loaded and stowed below deck as follows:-

	Tons	Cwts	Qrtrs	Stones
Oats	30	15	0	0
Turnips	20	14	1	0
Potatoes	5	0	0	0
Sundries	3	19	2	6
Total	60	8	3	6

The sundries included one ton of hides, skins, bogies and general empties including ale and oil barrels and siphons. There was also a side board and a piano.

The aft deck was entirely clear of cargo.

The fore deck contained seven packages of passengers' 'luggage in advance' and eleven small parcels stowed under the forecastle head on the starboard side.

Although it came from all over the Island the mail on this voyage was light, comprising of six baskets of parcels and eleven bags of letters. Of the letter bags, five were from Douglas, two from Ramsey and one each from Peel, Castletown, Port Erin and Port St. Mary. The mail was stowed under the forecastle head on the port side.

There were eleven half-boxes of fish, ten of

'At one a.m. in Ramsey Bay
Captain Teare was heard to say
'Our contract says deliver the mail
In this rough weather we must not fail'

'The Ellan Vannin Tragedy'
by Hughie Jones of The Spinners

THE SWING BRIDGE, RAMSEY, 1998.

cod and conger eels and one of sole stowed under the bridge.

As well as this inanimate cargo the *Ellan Vannin* carried a number of animals. One pig and 88 sheep were equally divided between pens on the port and starboard sides. There were three pens on either side of the foredeck with about 15 sheep in each. The weight on either side was not in excess of 45cwts. Although some horses were due to be carried, in the event, only the sheep and the pig were loaded that night.

The sun had set at 3.53pm and it is likely that some of the crew would have stayed on board, perhaps taking the opportunity for a sleep because they would be on duty for the night crossing. Indeed, one could well imagine that in the days when the steamer's boilers needed to be kept fired up, many of the crew may have been working in the engine room whilst others would be awaiting the arrival of the first passengers. Few of the crew would have been tempted to leave the warmth of the *Ellan Vannin* and go ashore on a cold December night.

High tide was at 2.59am, and when the *Ellan Vannin* had floated at 12.30am, she was perfectly upright, her draught forward being 7ft 6ins and aft 10ft.

The Captain, James Teare, and the Company's agent, James Bell, would have had the benefit of two sources of information about the weather, both of which were close by. Firstly, there was a barometer on the Custom House at the harbour's edge. The old Custom House on the East Quay is still there today with the mark where the barometer once hung still

The Isle of Man Steam Packet Company, Limited.

INCORPORATED IN THE ISLE OF MAN.

YOUR

Ramsey,

ISLE OF MAN

TELEGRAPHIC ADDRESS:
STEAMERS, RAMSEY, MAN.

190

All Traffic subject to the Conditions of Carriage of the Company,
as exhibited in their Offices and on board their Steamers,

Oats

R. Kneale	290 Sks Oats	21. 15. 0. 0
Farmers Combine	180 " "	9. 0. 0. 0
		30. 15. 0 0

Turnips

			Oats	30. 15. 0. 0	£00
T. P. Cowley	60 bags Turnips	6 5. 0. 0	Turnips	20 14. 1. 0	£14
R. Kneale	33 " "	2. 14. 0. 0	Potatoes	5. 0. 0	£10 10
Quayle	43 " "	2 17. 3. 0	Sundries	3 19. 2. 6	
Farmers Assn	55 " "	3 17. 0. 0.		1	
Belling	48 " "	4. 4. 1. 0	60. 8 3 6	
Quayle	13 " "	16. 1. 0		
		20 14. 1 0		

Potatoes

T. B. Cowley	60 bags Potatoes	4 0. 0. 0
Quayle	14 " "	1. 0. 0. 0
766		5. 0. 0

Live Stock.

R. E. Garrett to Smith	1 Pig
J. J. Christian " "	28 Sheep
R. Teare " "	19 "
J. Brown " "	9 "
C. & F. Crowe " "	32 "
	89

THE ELLAN VANNIN'S CARGO ON HER LAST VOYAGE. THE LIST WAS PRESUMABLY PREPARED BY THE STEAM PACKET'S RAMSEY AGENT, JAMES BELL.

visible. Secondly, the Coastguard's Office, which is still near the East Quay, would have displayed storm warning cones showing the wind's direction, the information having been telegraphed from Glasgow.

The barometer went down very low that night, and at one time registered 28.3. Such a low reading is very unusual. Between 6 and 7pm the wind had veered to the south-east with a strong breeze causing fairly heavy seas. There were violent showers. These conditions continued until approximately 8.30pm when they abated. About 10 or 10.30pm the wind changed round to the north-west and became lighter. At some time before departure, newspapers later reported, the Company's agent said to Captain Teare, 'It's going to be a dirty night' to which comment the Captain replied 'it looks like snow.' The Captain also said that he thought that as the wind was aft they'd have a good passage. Captain Teare's forecast of snow proved to be accurate because on the following morning at daylight both the Manx hills and those visible in England were snow-capped.

However, the nature of the adverse conditions of that night was illustrated by the fate of the coaster *Helen* taking a cargo of sand from Holyhead to Silloth at the mouth of the Solway Firth. Due to the weather the cargo had shifted and the Captain decided to put into Ramsey. The low tide and the *Helen*'s dangerous state caused her Captain to put the ship on the beach at about 10.30pm. Shortly afterwards, with the rising tide, she was refloated, and according to a report in an edition of the *Ramsey Courier and Northern Advertiser* the next day, the *Ellan Vannin* towed the coaster into Ramsey harbour before finally leaving for Liverpool. This must have been quite a risky operation to have undertaken in the dark with relatively heavy seas and a load of cargo and passengers. However, Lloyd's List in London, which is a daily record of all shipping events throughout the world, records that the

'*Helen* entered harbour at 11.30pm', in other words, an hour before the Ellan Vannin was reported as having floated. Like so many aspects of the reporting of this tragedy, contradictions abound.

Captain Teare was one of the most cautious of the Company's masters and he would be the last man to leave port if it was too dangerous to do so. At the subsequent Board of Trade enquiry it was accepted that there was nothing in the weather to indicate that it was unreasonable to leave Ramsey and there was no criticism of his decision to sail.

Although her scheduled departure time was 1.00am the *Ellan Vannin* began her last voyage a few minutes late at 1.13am. She was en route for Salisbury Dock, Liverpool, and there were to be no ports of call. The vessel was in perfect trim with plenty of freeboard as she was only carrying just over one quarter of her capacity.

Reginald R Bailey, later to be Lord Mayor of Liverpool, was holidaying with his father three months before the *Ellan Vannin* sank. His father knew the Captain and at Ramsey they went on board the *Ellan Vannin*. Mr Bailey recalled that the Captain said to him 'this brave little ship has done the run between

THE MENU AVAILABLE TO THE ELLAN VANNIN'S PASSENGERS.

STEWARDS' DEPARTMENT.

SALOON TARIFF.

	s.	d.
BREAKFAST (Plain)	1	0
,, with hot and cold		
meats	2	0
LUNCHEON	2	0
DINNER (5 Courses)	2	6
TEA (plain)	1	0
,, { with hot and cold meats	2	0
PLATE OF MEAT	1	0
CUP OF TEA OR COFFEE ...	0	4
SANDWICH	0	4
CUP OF TEA, with bread and		
butter	0	6
BISCUIT AND CHEESE ...	0	2
PLAIN BISCUITS	0	1
CAKES, assorted	0	2

FORE CABIN TARIFF.

BREAKFAST, DINNER, or TEA		
from ... ... 1/- to	1	6
CUP OF TEA	0	3
,, ,, with biscuits ...	0	4

WINES, &c.

CHAMPAGNE, per qrt....9/- & 10/6
,,   per pint 5/- & 5/6
BURGUNDY, per quart 4/- & 5/6
,,   per pint ...2/6 & 3/-
STILL HOCKS, per qrt. 3/- & 4/-
,,   per pint 2/- & 2/6
CLARETS, per quart ...3/- & 4/-
,,   per pint ...1/6 & 2/-
PORT & SHERRY... ... 5/-
,,   per pt. 2/6
LIQUEURS, per glass ... 6d.

	gls.	½-gls.
BRANDY	8d.	4d.
WHISKEY, Scotch & Irish	6d.	3d.
RUM, GIN, PORT, and		
SHERRY	6d.	3d.
BASS'S ALE ... per bot.	4d.	
GUINNESS'S STOUT ,,	4d.	
MINERAL WATERS—		
Schweppe's & Cantrell's	6d.	3d.
CIGARS ... ... each	4d.	6d.

Meals can be had at all times on the Steamer during passage.

PRIVATE or STATE CABINS.

Extra Charge: **7/6** each cabin, irrespective of number of passengers occupying them. No. 1 Cabins (large) on " Empress Queen," " Queen Victoria," and "Prince of Wales," are **10/-** each. These Cabins can be reserved at embarking ports, if not previously engaged.

THE JOURNEY

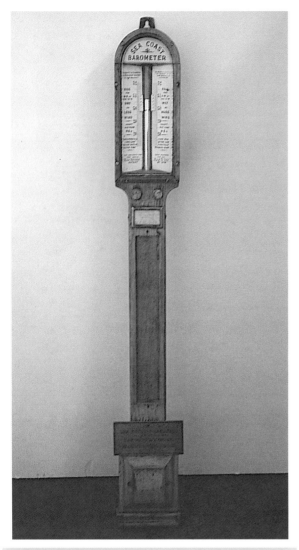

THE BAROMETER CONSULTED BY CAPTAIN TEARE BEFORE DEPARTURE FROM RAMSEY FOR THE LAST TIME. THE BAROMETER IS NOW IN THE HARBOUR MASTER'S OFFICE.

the Isle of Man and Liverpool so many times that while I am on the bridge I feel the *Ellan Vannin* could find the way to the Mersey if she was left to do it on her own.'

Captain Teare took the *Ellan Vannin* out of the harbour into the open sea, no doubt following the route that is followed today by the many captains that take the current vessels out of Ramsey harbour. At the time of sailing the wind was reported as continuing to be north-westerly but with a moderate breeze and heavy showers of sleet.

The Company's records show that the *Ellan Vannin* sailed from Ramsey with 14 passengers and 21 crew. Ramsey to Liverpool is approximately 85 miles and the estimated journey time was seven to eight hours. Whilst there is a recorded crossing time of six and a half hours by the *Ellan Vannin* the more usual time was seven hours and upwards.

Of the 14 passengers nine were in saloon accommodation and five in steerage. The total receipts for ticket sales from this journey were £2 11s. The 21 crew comprised ten in the deck department, seven in the engine department and four in the stewards' department.

It may be of interest to note that the Steam Packet Company's ships did not become one class for another 57 years. The *Ben-my-Chree V*, launched in December 1965, was the last of the Company's vessels to be built with passenger accommodation designed for two classes. The cost of the extra stewards and the equality conscious days of the late 1960s led to the Company's vessels becoming 'one class' ships with effect from 1st January 1967.

The helmsman stood at the wheel out in the open on a small deck in front of the room that housed the charts and the captain's cabin. The helmsman was often a senior deckhand or able seaman, and a watchman would also be on permanent duty. Usually the captain stood on the flying deck which was above and behind the wheel. Here the binnacle housing the compass and other instruments was placed. This would be lit by two special oil lamps during night sailings.

The captain could communicate with the engine room from the flying bridge down a talking tube and he could also give instructions to the helmsman just below him. In poor weather a canvass dodger would be strung up across part of the upper bridge to offer some protection from the wind and rain. In difficult conditions more than one man might be required to turn the wheel.

There is very little direct evidence of what happened on board the *Ellan Vannin* after she left Ramsey. The two potential sources of information about the ship's log, Lloyd's Marine Collection at the Guildhall Library in London, and the University of Newfoundland in Canada which holds 80% of ships'

20

THE ELLAN VANNIN STORY

THE JOURNEY

THE IRISH SEA GIVES A BATTERING TO QUEEN'S PROMENADE, RAMSEY.

logs for the period 1863—1938 have no record of the *Ellan Vannin*'s log. Unless it is in private hands, we must assume that it was never recovered from the wreck.

No detailed record remains of the precise weather information Captain Teare had before the *Ellan Vannin* left Ramsey on 3rd December 1909. As we have seen, Captain Teare would have had the benefit of knowing the general direction of unfavourable conditions by virtue of the storm warning cones at the Coastguard's Office. Met. Office records show that these cones were hoisted around the coast of Ireland, on the Isle of Man and on the Welsh coast, sometime after 7.00am on 2nd December, though the exact time is not recorded. It must be presumed that Captain Teare would have seen the warning cones after arriving in Ramsey to prepare for the late sailing.

At the subsequent Board of Trade enquiry into the loss of the *Ellan Vannin,* no criticism was made of Captain Teare's decision to sail. However, what is not clear, is whether the enquiry were aware that storm warning cones were flying in Ramsey, as this is not referred to.

The Assistant Harbour Master, John Callow, made two reports of the weather. Firstly, he recorded a moderate north-westerly breeze at 1am. Secondly, this wind was in the same direction and described as 'fresh, slightly increasing with showers of sleet' at 2.15am. Of course, words such as 'strong' and 'moderate' can be matters of opinion but there seems

little evidence to support the comments in the *Isle of Man Examiner* newspaper of 11th December 1909 that at departure time there was a 'strong north-westerly breeze'.

The *Examiner*'s report went on to say that an hour and a half into the voyage the wind increased considerably. The rising winds were reported as not being of concern to the Company because the wind was aft of the *Ellan Vannin* and the vessel had been in quite as bad, if not worse conditions, before. The source of the *Examiner*'s description of the weather is not known. Similarly the source of the Company's 'lack of concern' is not known. This reported lack of concern however, continued until much later in the day when the *Ellan Vannin* failed to arrive at Liverpool. Some newspapers reported that the wind had increased to almost tornado force by 2.45am (within one and a half hours of leaving Ramsey). The gusts were said to be the most severe for several years, causing the sea to run in the most fearful fashion. The source of information for these reports and their accuracy is not known but there can be no dispute that the winds came from the north-west and therefore, being behind the *Ellan Vannin*, would have caused less problems than if the ship had been travelling into the wind. Two further sources of information regarding the weather are available, from *The Times* and the Bidston Observatory in Birkenhead on Merseyside.

The Times' weather chart for 6.00pm on the 2nd December (seven hours before the *Ellan Vannin* sailed) showed that the Isle of Man was subject to a fresh or strong wind from a roughly south-westerly direction. The temperature was 51°F (11°C). There was no indication that a violent gale in the Irish Sea was expected but the general forecast was that there was a new depression in the west and that this was expected to move to the east or north-east. It was anticipated that strong winds or gales would be caused and these conditions were expected to bring with them squally, showery weather over England and Ireland and freshening winds in Scotland.

The Times' detailed weather forecast for the 24 hours ending at midnight Friday 3rd December (which covered the time the *Ellan Vannin* was at sea)

THE JOURNEY

THE ELLAN VANNIN LEAVING RAMSEY CARRYING TROOPS BACK TO ENGLAND.

stated that the conditions were expected to be:-

North-West England: wind mainly between south and west, fresh or strong; a gale in places; squally rain and a mild to moderate temperature.

Western Scotland: wind varying in both direction and force; showers of rain, sleet or snow with a rather cold temperature.

All Ireland: wind mainly between west and north-west or north, strong to a gale in places; squally showers of rain with moderate to rather low temperatures.

In summary, not the best conditions but not untypical of those frequently encountered by the *Ellan Vannin* on her crossings between the Island and Liverpool.

The Bidston Observatory at the Proudman

Oceanographic Laboratory is now under the responsibility of the Natural Environment Research Council. In 1909 Bidston was one of the weather stations for the north-west of England whose reports were used by the Met. Office in London. At that time some of Bidston's weather observations were made by a Canon Robson who was a vicar with a parish in Wallasey on the Wirral Peninsular at the mouth of the River Mersey. Canon Robson was also the weather correspondent for the *Liverpool Daily Post and Evening Express* newspaper.

At 8.00am on 3rd December, Canon Robson recorded a rainfall of 1.01 inches. Whilst there is no indication of the period covered, it is probably the total for the previous 24 hours. A rainfall of an inch or more in 24 hours is high and indicates heavy rain during the *Ellan Vannin*'s crossing.

THE JOURNEY

		Rain.	Sun	Temp	Min Grass	Bar	Wind	Force	Weather
Dec:	1	Nil	0.18	42		29.01	WSE	2	Unsettled
	2	0.29	Nil	40	34	29.22	SSW	1	fine
	3	1.05	1.0	36	32	28.29	NW	10	Dreadful Day
about 1½	4	0.59	0.30 ½.20	34	28	28.80	NW	3	cold miserable
	5	0.13	6.30	33	26	28.91	NW	2	Lovely
	6	0.28* Nil	small -0.00	32	26	28.90	SE	2	Snow!
	7	0.08* Nil	0.00*	32	26	29.10	SE	2	Sleet
	8	0.02 Nil	6.36	34	25	29.50	W	2	Lovely
	9	Nil	Nil	39	34	30.20	SSW	2	fine
	10	0.22	Nil	52	–	29.80	SSW	3	Rain
3.25	11	0.88	Nil	50	–	29.75	SSW	3	Rain
about 1½	12	0.09	Nil	44	–	30.00	E	2	fine
	13	Nil	Nil	42	–	30.30	NE	3	cold
	14	Nil	Nil	40	28	30.50	E	8	fine
	15	Nil	Nil	39	30	30.46	E	4	
2018	16	Nil	Nil	37	30	30.20	E	4	
	17	0.08	Nil	36	33	29.80	E		
	18	0.06	0.18	36	30	29			
snow	19	0.30*	Nil	28	20				
	20	0.70*	2.30	32	24				
	21	0.25*	4.36	24	10				
	22	0.10*	Nil	34	14	28			

T. Ellan Vannin Bank Passage boat sank

CANON ROBSON'S DIARY ENTRY FOR DECEMBER 1909. THE CANON WAS WEATHER OBSERVER FOR THE BIDSTON OBSERVATORY AND THE MET OFFICE. IN ADDITION TO HIS PARISH DUTIES IN WALLASEY, HE WAS ALSO THE WEATHER CORRESPONDENT FOR THE LIVERPOOL DAILY POST AND EVENING EXPRESS NEWSPAPER. THE SINKING OF THE ELLAN VANNIN IS NOTED AT THE BOTTOM OF THE PAGE.

THE JOURNEY

The air temperature was 36°F (2°C) and the lowest temperature in the period was 32°F (0°C). The barometer reading at 8.00am was 28.29 inches (958.0 millibars). A reading of 28.29 inches is a particularly low reading. Indeed, the Bidston Observatory's lowest ever reading was 27.75 inches (939.7 millibars) which was recorded in 1886. The Met. Office's annual weather summary for 1909 indicates that the cyclonic system of 2nd and 3rd December was the deepest of the year. However, forecasted conditions were expected to be much more benign. The Met. Office's forecast for the 24 hours from noon on 2nd December (13 hours before the *Ellan Vannin*'s departure) to noon on 3rd December (five hours after she sank) was:

'Variable breezes between south-west and north-west, light to moderate, but fresh at times locally; changeable, some rain; temperature moderate to cool.'

Canon Robson's records show the wind at 8.00am on 3rd December as blowing from a north-westerly direction. Contrary to the forecasts, he observed the wind as being of storm force 10 on the Beaufort Scale. Canon Robson went on to describe the weather as 'dreadful'. His records for 3rd December were later noted to record '*Ellan Vannin* Manx passenger boat sunk'.

A forecast is just that, and of course, it can be wrong. Nevermore so than on the day the *Ellan Vannin* sailed for the last time. By the time of the next daily Met. Office report and forecast (7.00am, 3rd December) the *Ellan Vannin* was either sunk or sinking. This report described the very rough weather experienced over much of the United Kingdom on the previous night. Heavy rain had fallen generally. The inch in Liverpool, reported by Canon Robson being specifically referred to. Wireless transmissions from ships reported westerly and north-westerly winds from force 6 to a whole gale as far west as the 18th Meridian (to the west of Ireland).

The Bidston Observatory recorded the wind details by using a Dines pressure tube anometer. Up until 2.30am on 3rd December the mean wind speed averaged 25 miles per hour. On the Beaufort Scale this

	Beaufort Scale of Wind force for use on sea	Equivalent speed	
Beaufort Number		mph.	knots
6	Strong breeze. Large waves begin to form; the white foam crests are more extensive everywhere. Probably some spray.	25-31	22-27
7	Near gale. Sea heaps up and white foam from breaking waves begins to be blown in streaks along direction of the wind.	32-38	28-33
8	Gale Moderately high waves of greater length; edges of crests begin to break into spindrift. The foam is blown in well-marked streaks alongthe direction of the wind.	39-46	34-40
9	Strong gale. High waves. Dense streaks of foam along the direction of the wind. Crests of waves begin to topple, tumble and roll over. Spray may affect visibility.	47-54	41-47
10	Storm. Very high waves with long overhanging crests. The resulting foam, in great patches, is blown in dense white streaks along the direction of the wind. On the whole the surface of the sea takes a white appearance. The 'tumbling' of the sea becomes heavy and shock-like. Visibility affected.	55-63	48-55
11	Violent storm. Exceptionally high waves (small and medium sized ships might be for a time lost to view behind the waves). The sea is completely covered with long white patches of foam lying along the direction of the wind. Everywhere the edges of the wave crests are blown into froth. Visibility affected	64-72	56-63
12	Hurricane. The air is filled with foam and spray. Sea completely white with driving spray; visibility very seriously affected.	73-82	64-71

equates to wind force 6 characterised by a strong breeze with large waves beginning to form. The speed of such a storm is 25 to 31 miles per hour or 22 to 27 knots. However, the weather worsened quite quickly. At 2.30am there was a sudden sharp increase in wind speed to 45 miles per hour which indicates the upper end of a gale force 8 with moderately high waves and breaking crests. The mean wind speed then increased steadily to 65 miles per hour by 4.00am. A wind speed of 65 miles per hour is a storm force 11 which is a violent storm with excpetionally high waves during which (the Beaufort Scale description says) 'small and medium sized ships might be for a time lost to view behind the waves'.

Half an hour later the storm was at its height. The Bidston Observatory recorded the wind speed as 81 miles an hour at about 4.35am. A wind speed of 81 miles per hour is equivalent, on the Beaufort Scale, to force 12 - a hurricane. Hurricane force winds are rarely experienced in the British Isles. After this extreme, at 4.35am, the wind decreased slowly to be a strong gale of force 9.

It is fairly unusual for Bidston Observatory to record a force nine gale. This only occurs about once a year and is usually recorded less often than that. It is extremely rare for the Bidston Observatory to record a mean wind speed of force 10 or 11. At the height of the storm, force 12 winds were recorded. Force 12 conditions are virtually unknown at Bidston.

Although the Bidston Observatory's recordings were of the weather in Birkenhead on Merseyside and not of conditions out on the Irish Sea, they are the most accurate available that might indicate the kind of weather the *Ellan Vannin* encountered on her crossing. It is reasonable to assume that the wind speeds described would have been experienced over much of north-west England and the Isle of Man as well as on the Irish Sea between the Manx and English coasts.

As the gale was blowing from the north-west it would have reached the *Ellan Vannin* before reaching the Bidston Observatory. This means it is probable that the *Ellan Vannin,* part-way through its journey, would have encountered conditions of Beaufort force 8 (gale force) at around 2.00am. In other words the

weather conditions recorded at the Bidston Observatory would have reached the *Ellan Vannin* about 30 minutes before they reached Bidston. The 30 minutes would have progressively lessened as the *Ellan Vannin* approached Liverpool and got closer to Bidston. Whilst this is still an assumption, this would mean that the *Ellan Vannin* would have encountered the most ferocious of the winds (namely the maximum of 81 miles per hour - hurricane or force 12 winds) at approximately 4.15am.

Unlike today's Steam Packet vessels the Ellan Vannin was not in contact with any source of weather information, as there was no ship-to-shore communication. The question therefore arises of whether Captain Teare should have decided not to press on to his intended destination of Liverpool. Suggestions have been made that the Ellan Vannin should have turned back for Ramsey. However, a moment's reflection will indicate that to turn back would have been fool-hardy as the wind was coming from the north-west. To turn back would have meant heading into the gale. Every captain would have taken a similar decision to Captain Teare's, namely, that it would have been better to proceed with the wind behind you rather than trying to turn broadside and travel back into the gale.

Other commentators maintained that Captain Teare could have considered not proceeding but that somehow he should have made for shelter. However, it is quite clear that there was no shelter to be found in the middle of the Irish Sea on that night! Others suggested that Captain Teare should have headed for the shelter of the Lancashire coast, but there was no guarantee that a change of course would have led to better weather. Further, such a course would have taken the *Ellan Vannin* in an easterly direction. To turn, albeit slightly into the wind, would have been unwise.

In all probability, the captain would not have made a conscious decision to continue, there was in fact no other choice. Indeed, Captain Teare may not have been unnecessarily concerned about continuing. His ship was well crewed, had few passengers, was carrying a light load, and must have experienced these kind of conditions many times on the crossing to and from the Isle of Man. It is worth noting that his

THE BAHAMA BANK LIGHTSHIP NORTH OF RAMSEY

decision to continue to Liverpool was never criticised by authoritative commentators.

There were numerous disasters to the shipping around the coasts of the United Kingdom due to the storms that night. Inland, telegraph wires were blown down and there was considerable damage to property. The large quantity of rain caused widespread flooding.

In the north-west the torpedo boat *066* went ashore on the West Barrow Sands. No part of the coast seemed to escape. In the south-west the Albyn Line steamer *Thistlemor*, en route from Cardiff to South Africa, was wrecked off the north Devonshire coast with the loss of 21 lives. The *Thistlemor* was a new vessel of over 4,000 tons gross (ten times that of

the *Ellan Vannin*), but even she could not escape the ravages of the weather on 3rd December 1909.

In the English Channel numerous vessels were smashed by the seas. Near Eastbourne the steamer *Eastfield* went ashore. At Dover a Turkish steamer was driven ashore, and further round the coast at Sheerness, the battleship *Implacable* and a cruiser broke adrift from their harbour moorings and were driven ashore.

As the conditions deteriorated after the *Ellan Vannin*'s departure there was considerable damage to buildings. In Ramsey, for example, the Vicarage at May Hill had some of its stonework displaced. The wind lifted the glass off the body of the frame used by the Reverend Devall for growing plants and deposited it some distance away. Ramsey was not the only town to suffer. The storm interfered with the Island's telephone wires and by morning many connections were down.

There is a newspaper report that the crew of the nearby Bahama Bank Lightship described the weather as storm force 11 in the early hours of the morning of 3rd December. However, the lightship's weather records, which have been preserved by the Met. Office, do not contain any information concerning the wind speed or direction. It is therefore not possible to confirm the newspaper's report. If the lightship's records were more detailed, one other vital piece of information would have been available: the precise weather conditions when the *Ellan Vannin* left Ramsey. The lightship was only a few miles from Ramsey and the weather conditions would have been similar in both locations.

In the same way it is not certain whether the Board of Trade enquiry was aware storm warning cones were flying in Ramsey, there is no indication as to whether the enquiry considered calling witnesses from the Bahama Bank Lightship. Such witnesses would have been able to provide crucial evidence about the weather at the time of Captain's Teare's decision to sail, as well as that experienced by the ship in the first few hours of its last voyage.

The night sailing in the opposite direction, from Liverpool to Douglas, was being undertaken by the *Fenella* and she left at 11.40pm on 2nd December in what were said to be severe weather conditions.

THE JOURNEY

Thirteen miles from the docks in Liverpool she would have passed the Bar Lightship, the crew of which was to give important evidence at the later Board of Trade enquiry. These curious vessels, which were permanently manned, were anchored in one place. As the name implies, their purpose was to light the location of a particular hazard to shipping. The Bar Lightship indicated to approaching ships that they were at the sandbank or shoal at the mouth of the River Mersey - the 'bar'. A river always brings silt and stones down with it, and at the point where the river's energy is finally absorbed by the sea, a ridge of stones and silt can build up. This is called the bar, and constant dredging is often required to ensure a safe channel for shipping. These days, rather than a manned lightship, a light buoy is usually employed to show various hazards such as banks of sand below the surface.

Records from the Bar Lightship accord with those of the Bidston Observatory a few miles away. A heavy gale had sprung up at about 4.00am when the wind was force 11. The wind came from a north-westerly direction. The lightship's log showed that at 6.00am the weather was still very violent, only just below hurricane force. The visibility was poor with cloud, mist and hail. There were exceptionally heavy squalls in the rough sea. These conditions continued until 8.00am.

Numerous captains described the conditions at the time as 'the most awful storm through which he'd sailed', or 'a gale raging like a wild cat'. However, perhaps the most accurate account of the weather faced by Captain Teare and the *Ellan Vannin* comes from the Captain of the *Heroic*. The *Heroic*, a twin screw steamer, was travelling from Belfast bound for Liverpool and passed the Bar just before 6.00am. The ship's master, Captain Porter, described the storm as being of extraordinary violence with the wind being a fierce hurricane from the north-west. The channels and banks were swept by a terrific sea. The waves were at a height of 24 feet. The wind and seas were the worst he had ever experienced in the vicinity. He had 11 years experience of these waters.

At the lightship itself, shortly after 6.30am, an inward bound steamer passed about half a mile northwards. The steamer's masthead light was seen for about five minutes, until becoming obscured by a heavy shower. Taking into consideration the time usually taken by the *Ellan Vannin* on her journey from Ramsey to Liverpool to that point, and the direction in which the steamer was approaching the Bar, there is every possibility that the light seen was that of the *Ellan Vannin*.

At the time the *Ellan Vannin* arrived at the bar the tide would have been at its hardest ebb. The sea that had flooded up the River Mersey was now returning and at 6.30am, which was three and a half hours after high tide, this huge volume of water met almost hurricane force winds driving in the opposite direction which created waves of 25ft, and probably more. The *Ellan Vannin* was also at the most dangerous part of the channel, where it was narrow and shallow, factors which only served to increase the violence and force of the waves.

At approximately 6.45am, Williams, one of the seamen on the Bar Lightship, saw what he described as a flash, coloured green with a greenish tinge, lasting about a second. The flash was in the vicinity of the Bar and from the direction in which the steamer had gone. The seaman alerted the Master of the lightship. The Master and the seaman spent about 20 minutes looking out for any further signs. They thought the flash was a signal from a vessel and a second signal would have confirmed that she was in distress, but no further flash was seen. The crew of the lightship had prepared the signals to summon lifeboats from the neighbouring shores but after a while, not seeing a second signal, they did nothing more. At about this time the chart at the Bar Lightship recorded the weather as being one point below hurricane force.

The *Ellan Vannin*'s clock was later discovered to have stopped at 6.50am, and as the ship was found in the same vicinity as the lone flash observed by the seaman, it was taken as confirmation that what he had seen were the last moments of the sinking ship. Although there were a number of steamers bound both inward and outward that morning, principally on the Ireland-England routes, no one else reported seeing the *Ellan Vannin*.

At the time there was much debate concerning the cause of the flash. It is possible that it was caused by the boiler bursting as it was swamped by the sea, but noted engineers commented that there were

THE JOURNEY

approximately 60 feet of tubes between the ship's boiler and the funnel. Any flash from a sudden onrush of water would have to travel a considerable distance to be seen on the surface. Technically, so the engineers said, a flash could not travel this distance through the tubes.

It was possible, of course, that it was a distress flare, and during evidence later reported from the Board of Trade Enquiry, it was stated that what had been seen was a 'flare-up in the vicinity of the Bar for about a minute'. This contradicted previous evidence that what had been seen was a flash which lasted for only a second and so no definitive answer was arrived at as to what had actually caused the flash or flare.

Ironically, at the time the *Ellan Vannin* sank, a lifeboat was only a short distance away. At about 6.30am the New Brighton lifeboat had gone to a Liverpool bound steamer, the *Billacio*, which was believed to be in trouble. Although the lifeboat passed about a mile from where the *Ellan Vannin* sank, the poor visibility or the lack of any distress signals meant the lifeboat's crew saw nothing. The *Billacio*'s Captain told the lifeboat his ship was in good order and he did not need assistance.

Area

British Isles, Irish Sea, southern and central latitudes of the North Sea and its coasts, by the latter half of the day the Southern Baltic as well; also the European plain and adjacent areas from North France to North Germany.

Observations

There were many shipwrecks and many lives lost as a very deep depression crossed Ireland and then Northern England, with central pressures down to about 948 mb at the deepest phase. It then continued northeast across the North Sea to be centred over South Norway on the morning of the 4th.

Gales force 8 from between WSW and WNW were blowing over much of England on the 3rd and force 10 from these directions were reported over the southern North Sea, the Channel and the Bay of Biscay. The gale on the 3rd began as a SE'ly generally

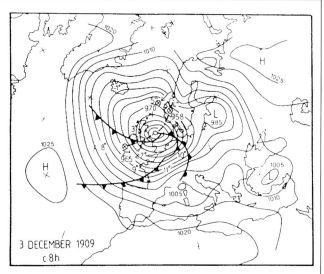

3 DECEMBER 1909 c 8h

force 8 to 9 over Denmark and force 10 SE'ly at the coast of southwest Norway.

CHAPTER FOUR

THE PASSENGERS

Early reports of the *Ellan Vannin* disaster gave the number of passengers carried as twelve and this was the figure reported in London by *The Times* the day after the tragedy.

The Company agent's receipts for tickets sold, and the returns of the passenger names show that there were, in fact, fourteen passengers that died that night. Although a relatively small number in terms of the vessel's maximum capacity, it is interesting that long before the days of computerisation, such an accurate record of passenger numbers and their identification was available.

The following passengers were aboard the *Ellan Vannin* when she sailed:

Mark Henry Joughin

Mark Henry Joughin, aged 44.
Truro Cottage, Bride.

Mr Joughin was a farmer and Wesleyan lay preacher whose services were much in demand. He

'Through well-nigh half a century of life
She battled bravely 'mid the ocean's strife,
And now, like many a veteran beside,
Amid the roar of battle has she died!
Fourteen passengers were lost,
In the dreadful seas they were tossed.'

- W. Gell (amended)

was unmarried and lived with his mother, who was nearly eighty, and his two sisters. He was planning to sail by the Cunard liner *Campania* from Liverpool to New York the next day, Saturday 4th December. Newspapers later reported that he was on his way to America to claim a fortune that had been left to him by his uncle. It was said that never more true was the expression 'to him that hath all shall be given,' because Mr Joughin was already reasonably well off.

Further, popular belief may not be absolutely accurate. Whilst he had been to America before in connection with his supposed fortune, an article in the *Manx Quarterly* of April 1910, claimed that it had been left to his mother by her brother, the late William Cain. William Cain was formerly of Kirk Michael but, at the time of his death, he owned an estate near Minneapolis, Minnesota worth about £30,000. The acres of timber and the railways which ran through the estate contributed to its value. It seems, therefore, that Mr Joughin was in fact on his way to America to deal with his mother's inheritance.

A young relative of his had a premonition of the forthcoming disaster. He dreamt that Mark Joughin was praying with others in the *Ellan Vannin*'s saloon. He woke his mother and told her what he had seen. She comforted him and, as mothers do, told him to 'go back to sleep'. The dream took place some four hours before the disaster. Premonitions might have been a Joughin family trait. When Mark Joughin preached in Bride two Sundays before his death, in the course of his sermon he used the words, 'We are blind, we are very blind. We cannot see very far ahead'.

According to the Steam Packet agent's record of ticket sales and passengers, Mr Joughin owned sufficient shares in the Steam Packet Company to be entitled to a free passage on the *Ellan Vannin*, although, for some reason, neither he nor anyone else living at his address is shown in the Steam Packet's official share register as a shareholder.

Mrs John Allen and her son Ernest, aged 16.
Hawthorn Cottage, Maughold and 14, Slater Street, Liverpool.

Mrs Allen was a Sunday school teacher at St.

THE PASSENGERS

Luke's Church at the top of Bold Street, Liverpool, and Ernest sang in the choir. Mr Allen was in business as a plumber and paint manufacturer in Liverpool, and the family spent much of the summer and odd weekends during the rest of the year at Hawthorn Cottage in Maughold. The attractive cottage, in a peaceful location near to Maughold Church, must have been a welcome retreat from busy suburban Liverpool, and they were frequent travellers from Liverpool to Ramsey. Mr Allen had bought the cottage two years previously.

Mrs Allen and Ernest had come to Ramsey in November to look at an extension that had been added to the cottage. Mr Allen received a letter from his son to say that they were coming back on the *Ellan Vannin*. Mother and son arrived in Ramsey on the tram at 9.15pm. They travelled on the Steam Packet with a contract ticket. It is likely that they travelled in a first class saloon cabin.

THE TRAFALGAR HOTEL AS IT IS TODAY. IN 1909 MR HIGGINBOTHAM WAS THE LICENSEE. HE WAS TRAVELLING ON THE ELLAN VANNIN TO SEEK MEDICAL ADVICE IN MANCHESTER.

William Edward Higginbotham

William Edward Higginbotham.
Trafalgar Hotel, Ramsey.

Mr Higginbotham lived in the Trafalgar Hotel, Ramsey, and was its tenant. He was married with two children, a son and a daughter. He was formerly a draper in Douglas and had lived for many years at Primrose Cottage, Richmond Hill, on the outskirts of Douglas. When his health failed he took on the tenancy of the Trafalgar and as a result he became a well-known public

figure in Ramsey. He was also an influential member of the Licensed Victuallers' Association.

Newspaper reports claim that on the day of his departure on the *Ellan Vannin* he made his will. He obtained a witness and signature. His will was carefully concealed in the pocket of a coat, which he left at the hotel. However, the probate records in the Manx Museum reveal he died intestate. For some reason the will must have been invalid.

He was bound for Withington, Manchester, to see a medical man about his ill-health. He had made his will because he feared he may not return. The Trafalgar Hotel is only a few hundred yards from where the *Ellan Vannin* was berthed and we can assume that Mr Higginbotham probably 'called time' in the usual way before he left. He travelled on a return first-class saloon ticket, which cost ten shillings.

Miss Louis Findlay, aged 21.
83 Gray Hill Road, Well Hill, Eltham, Kent.

Miss Findlay was in the service of Mrs MacClennan of Ealing, London. Mrs MacClennan

usually used a house in Castletown when visiting the Island but on this occasion it was let to someone else. She therefore took a house in Brookfield Drive, Ramsey. Miss Findlay was leaving the Island to visit her sick brother, and had her mistress not left Castletown it is unlikely she would have sailed from Ramsey, but instead would have used Douglas. She travelled on the return part of what could have been a through railway ticket. It is likely that she travelled in steerage accommodation.

The circumstances of Miss Findlay's departure on the *Ellan Vannin* gave rise to much speculation after the tragedy: was there an unknown female passenger still unaccounted for? Early reports said that two young females, identities unknown, were aboard, and these gave rise to this belief. One was soon found to be Miss Findlay, but who was the other? Many people saw two young females on board the ship before she sailed and a company official, the watchman, who punched tickets on the quayside, seems to have fuelled the rumours. For this sailing the watchman, it is believed, was Mr Thomas Killip of Church Street, Ramsey. The watchman later recalled receiving a ticket or tickets from one of the females for punching. He punched with one nip of his machine but could not say if he punched one or two tickets. Seeing two persons seems to have led to the belief that there were two passengers.

In fact what had happened was that Miss Findlay was seen off by another servant, Miss Lay. Miss Lay remained on board the *Ellan Vannin* for about one and a half hours. During this period of time many saw the couple on board. However, no one saw Miss Lay leave the ship, which gave rise to the rumour of the unknown female passenger until she came foward to clarify the situation.

Daniel Newall, aged about 60.
67, Hampton Road, Croydon, Surrey.

Mr Newall was a stone-mason who had been working on the new Roman Catholic church of Our Lady and St. Maughold which was under construction during 1909. He was returning to England. He was a widower with one son.

He had a single first-class saloon ticket, which

THE ROMAN CATHOLIC CHURCH IN RAMSEY. TWO OF THE ELLAN VANNIN'S PASSENGERS HELPED BUILD THE CHURCH AND THEY WERE RETURNING HOME TO ENGLAND.

cost six shillings. Clearly it was not only builders in the property boom of the 1980s who could afford to travel first-class!

Walter Williams, aged about 40.
12, Walgrove Terrace, Earl's Court Road, London.

Mr Williams was also a stone-mason working on the same church. He was married but with no children and was returning to England. He also travelled by single first-class saloon ticket.

Mrs Williams did not know that her husband had left Ramsey until she was told of the tragedy by a reporter from the *Star* newspaper in London.

Christopher Thomas Heaton Johnson, aged about 35, and Mrs Heaton Johnson.
Beaconsfield Towers, Jurby Road, Ramsey.

Mr Heaton Johnson was a civil servant working in India, where he held the important post of Assistant Commissioner in the Madras Presidency. He came to Ramsey in May on extended leave, with his wife and three children. He was a graduate of Cambridge University and a member of an old Lancastrian family. His grandfather was Dr James Johnson of Hampson, tutor of Professor Frankland and other distinguished physicists. He was said to be a man of kindly bearing and courteous disposition who had many friends in Ramsey.

Christopher Thomas Heaton Johnson

Mrs Heaton Johnson

Beaconsfield Towers today is an attractive residential home in spacious grounds. One can imagine that in the early twentieth century it would have had sufficient prestige for a government official, with his background, to live in whilst on leave. Mrs Heaton Johnson was related to the Marsh family who owned Beaconsfield Towers. Captain Marsh was a founder shareholder and director of the Isle of Man Bank.

Mr Heaton Johnson was returning to Madras, and early newspaper reports suggested that he was to travel on a Bibby liner from Liverpool the next day. However, he was in fact intending to spend a week in London before continuing to Madras. He wanted to be in Wimbledon before nightfall on 3rd December and so he caught the *Ellan Vannin* to be certain of getting an early train from Liverpool to London. He sailed from from Ramsey with his wife, who was intending to see him off from Liverpool.

After any disaster there are tales of 'what if?' Most of these can be disregarded with the benefit of hindsight, but in the case of the Heaton Johnsons such speculation is warranted. Contemporary newspapers reported that Mr Heaton Johnson tried to persuade his wife not to travel with him. Never could his wife's response have been more prophetic - 'No, I'd better see the last of you. You might get drowned you know.'

Their three children were left in the charge of Mrs Heaton Johnson's sister, Mrs Lambert, who also

had the assistance of an Indian nurse. Mr Heaton Johnson had a single, first-class saloon ticket, which cost six shillings. Mrs Heaton Johnson had a return first-class saloon ticket, which cost ten shillings.

Mrs William Crix

Mrs William Crix, nee Amy Moore, aged 23, plus infant, aged about 10 months. College Street, Ramsey.

Mrs Crix had been married for about a year to William Crix, a Ramsey fisherman, although she was a native of Liverpool. Mr Crix's family lived in what is now Old Post Office Lane, running from the harbourside to Parliament Street. Many residents in Ramsey still refer to this lane as Crix's Lane. Before her marriage Mrs Crix had been a servant at the Saddle

THE PASSENGERS

Hotel, which used to front onto Market Place in Ramsey.

Newspapers reported that she and her young child were on their way to see her father in England. However, others in Ramsey claimed that she was not just going to see her father, but was in fact leaving the Isle of Man altogether, having separated from her husband. This rumour was supported by the fact that she only bought a single steerage ticket for the crossing which cost three shillings and sixpence.

Miss Eleanor Fisher

Miss Eleanor (Nellie) Fisher, aged about 30.
Queen's Hotel, Ramsey.

Miss Fisher lived at the Queen's Hotel where she was head waitress and had worked for the previous five seasons. The hotel used to be just opposite the entrance to the Queen's Pier but was burned down in 1983.

Early reports said that she was on her way to a position in England. She had a brother and a daughter, aged seven, who lived in Ramsey. Her mother was an inmate of the Braust Charity Cottages in Ramsey. Her father, a former jobbing gardener in Ramsey, was dead. Despite her family connections and the fact that she was a well-known and trusted domestic servant, Miss Fisher decided to leave Ramsey.

To give some precision to the early reports, she was in fact going to see her sister in Runcorn before looking for work in England. Many friends saw her off, as the hotel was only a few minutes walk from the harbour. She had a single steerage ticket which cost three shillings and sixpence.

A postcript to these details has been provided by Miss Fisher's granddaughter, Mrs Duggan from Liverpool. Miss Fisher was an unmarried mother and her daughter suffered from the stigma of being illegitimate. However, a totally unexpected surprise happened when her daughter was 21. The local bank manager called her in and gave her a cheque for £100. The Fund established for the dependants of the *Ellan Vannin* disaster had allocated a weekly sum for her upbringing. This would seem never to have been claimed, or if claimed, had been left to accrue with interest. The daughter retained an affection for Ramsey where she later married and lived very happily.

Edgar John Blevin

Edgar John Blevin, aged 32.
21 Vaughan Road, New Brighton, Cheshire.

Mr Blevin was a prize-winning incorporated accountant. He had a wife and two young children. He had spent some years on the West Coast of Africa and when he came to the Island he worked for the accountants Kerruish & Sons who had branches in Douglas and Liverpool. Shortly after joining the partnership, which became Kerruish, Sons and Blevin in 1909, he was put in charge of the Liverpool branch

THE PASSENGERS

in Cook Street. He was popular with his fellow accountants, who spoke of his great ability and courteous manner. His knowledge of the Companies Acts and law was unequalled on the Island and he assisted in compiling the legislation in this area. He was described as a capable businessman with one of the most brilliant minds in Athol Street.

He was a busy man. He used to cross to the Island on a Tuesday to take evening classes in Douglas in book-keeping, which were full to capacity. Although there were daily crossings from Douglas to Liverpool, he usually returned on the *Ellan Vannin*'s 1.00am Friday sailing from Ramsey. On this occasion he left Douglas on the last tram at 8.00pm arriving in Ramsey at 9.15pm.

Mr Blevin travelled on a contract ticket which was the Steam Packet's equivalent of a railway season ticket. It is likely that he travelled in a first-class saloon cabin.

Although at first it was thought that Mr Blevin had not travelled on the *Ellan Vannin*, the son of the licensee of the Prince of Wales Hotel in Ramsey saw a businessman in the vessel's saloon before she sailed. The man had a tuft of dark hair hanging over his forehead. This tuft was particularly remarked upon by Mr Blevin's partners. Absolute confirmation came when his body was found.

Thomas Henry Quayle

Thomas Henry Quayle, aged 46.
Pear Tree Cottage, Andreas.

Mr Quayle is referred to in some reports as William Quayle. He was born in Andreas and was a former steward to the Venerable Archdeacon of Man. He was married with two daughters. A third daughter was born after his death. He was due to take up a position as the manager of church lands in Andreas - probably in the New Year of 1910.

He was a prominent member of the Andreas Society. His absence from an important sports committee meeting on Thursday 2nd December (the day before sailing) was remarked on. He was also helping to organise a concert for Ramsey Cottage Hospital which was to be held on the following Thursday. The concert, by the Andreas Male Voice Choir did in fact take place, but the beneficiaries were the dependants of those lost on the *Ellan Vannin*.

He was going to Liverpool to seek treatment for a cancerous growth in one of his ears. Mr Quayle was reluctant to talk about his movements to seek medical help.

It seems that Mr Quayle initially abandoned his intent to travel on the *Ellan Vannin* because of the bad weather on the Thursday evening. He retired to bed at 10.00pm, but got up at midnight and, finding that the weather had moderated, he cycled the five miles or so to Ramsey and caught the 1.00a.m. sailing. Never can a change of mind have been so costly. He travelled on a return steerage ticket which cost six shillings.

The approaching storm into which the *Ellan Vannin* sailed seems to have been responsible for persuading a number of people not to travel on that fateful night. Many later recalled their close brush with death, and there were others who, through some twist of fate or apparent premonition, were also spared.

Some of the accounts subsequently reported in the newspapers were somewhat fanciful, such as that of a friend of Mr Newall, one of the passengers, who was supposed to have spun a coin to decide whether to travel or not. As a result of the toss he did not go, but other accounts have at least a ring of truth about them.

One such is that of Harry Kaighin of Ballamin. He was a friend of Mark Joughin, who did sail on the *Ellan Vannin* and who was intending to travel on from Liverpool to America. In fact, both men were due to

THE PASSENGERS

travel on the Cunard liner *Campania* from Liverpool to New York on Saturday 4th December. The fortunate Harry Kaighin decided not to travel on the *Ellan Vannin* in view of the inclement weather. Instead, he took the Thursday night electric tram to Douglas, where his sister lived, said goodbye to her and caught the Friday morning boat to Liverpool where he had arranged to meet Mark Joughin. He did not find his friend at the meeting place, or at what he thought would be his hotel. He was thunder-struck when he read the reports of the disappearance of the *Ellan Vannin* and how close he had come to death.

The Kaighin family also escaped another loss. Harry's father is reported to have been intending to travel on the *Ellan Vannin* but he also decided that the weather was too rough. It is not known whether father and son spoke to each other about their intentions not to sail, and there appear to be no further details of the reason for Mr Kaighin senior travelling to Liverpool or whether he did so by another sailing.

Miss Weldhen was also spared due to the impending storm. She was originally from Liverpool but she lived in Ramsey, as her father had a piano tuning business in both places. In 1909 she was aged ten and had crossed to Ramsey on the *Ellan Vannin* with her brother and sister about ten days before 3rd December. The family planned to return to Liverpool on the *Ellan Vannin* on the 3rd, and they had loaded a piano and a sideboard, but because of the bad weather they decided not to sail, but left the furniture to go on ahead.

After the *Ellan Vannin* sank, the piano was found floating in the sea and Mr Weldhen subsequently had it repaired. It was then displayed in Hartley's Auction Room in London Road, Liverpool, where it could be viewed on payment of a small sum. The monies raised were paid to the Fund which was established for the dependants of those who died in the sinking.

Another passenger who was deterred from travelling on the *Ellan Vannin* by the strong weather was the Reverend H T Devall. Reverend Devall was the vicar of St. Paul's Church, a few yards from Ramsey harbour. He was due to sail to Liverpool to

take the place of the Reverend Adams, a minister of St. Augustine's Church in Liverpool but decided to take another sailing.

Another passenger who took a similar decision was Mr S H Marsden, the son of the licensee of the Prince of Wales Hotel in Ramsey. The hotel, which has now been converted into a block of residential flats of the same name, was a few yards from the harbour's edge. Mr Marsden went on board the *Ellan Vannin* shortly before the 1.00am departure but changed his mind on seeing the strong weather and came ashore again. Mr Marsden later gave evidence that identified one of the passengers, Mr Blevin, as being the man he had seen in the saloon of the *Ellan Vannin* before she sailed.

There were other passengers such as Major Banaster who intended to cross but, having arrived at the harbour, decided not to brave the elements, and a Miss Moore of Water Street, Ramsey, boarded the vessel but decided not to sail on account of the weather.

Some people avoided the sailing for reasons other than the weather, and one of the more interesting accounts of being spared from that fateful last crossing came in a letter to the *Liverpool Express and Echo* of 22nd April 1959, from a Mr T Shipsides of 42, Hogarth Road, Liverpool. Mr Shipsides joined the *Ellan Vannin* in August 1903 as a steward. A few days before 3rd December 1909, he was overcome by fear as to what was going to happen and he signed off the *Ellan Vannin*. Another crewman took his place and lost his life. At first sight this might seem a fanciful account, but it is interesting to consider that Mr Shipsides' recollection did not dim, to the extent that, nearly fifty years later, he was able to recall his feelings and write to his local paper about it.

Another crew member was also spared. Mr Fogerty had been the *Ellan Vannin*'s chief steward until a week before the disaster. The explanation given as to why Mr Fogerty did not sail on the *Ellan Vannin* was that he had been married recently under 'extraordinary circumstances'. In fact, Mr Fogerty's first wife had only recently died and his re-marriage on the Sunday before the *Ellan Vannin* sailed caused a local sensation. His actions were regarded as outrageous. Ever mindful of public opinion the Steam Packet suspended Mr

THE PASSENGERS

Fogerty. He was replaced at the last moment.

John Thomas Radcliffe, a Ramsey stock dealer and experienced sailor, was so concerned about the weather that night, that he decided against sending his shipment of cattle across. His fear was that the stormy weather could cause injury to the animals during the long journey.

The case of Mr Black illustrates that, despite the passage of time, the *Ellan Vannin* disaster had such an impact on Manx people that the tragedy is still referred to many years afterwards. In the *Isle of Man Weekly Times* newspaper of Tuesday 24th November 1981, a Mrs Greirson of Halifax in Yorkshire reminisced about the *Ellan Vannin* and her great-grandfather, whom she knew as 'Old Da Black'. She was a Black before getting married and the family home was Archdeacon Close, a farm in the north of the Island. Mr Black followed the practice of many men. He worked on the farm in the summer and in the winter he left his wife to run the farm whilst he went to sea. In the winter of 1909, Mr Black secured a position in the engine room of the *Ellan Vannin* and his first sailing was to have been on 3rd December.

He set out on foot for Ramsey and then fate intervened. On his way he met a friend who was driving a steam engine and Mr Black was glad to accept the offer of a lift.

Mr Black liked a drink and the first public house the two friends passed was the Ginger Hall in Sulby. The steam engine, so the couple later said, needed to take on frequent supplies of water and they applied the saying, 'let's have one for the road' too literally, stopping for a drink in every public house from the Ginger Hall to Ramsey harbour. As the pair finally approached the Central Hotel, close by the

harbour, they heard a ship's hooter. It was the *Ellan Vannin*'s final hooting before she sailed. Mr Black had arrived too late to work on the ship. He cannot have known how fortunate he was as he watched the ship's lights as she made her way out of the harbour for the last time.

Finally, the case of John Lewin can be added as a footnote. He was a prominent advocate on the Island who practised from Athol Street in Douglas. His father was also well known in Douglas, where he was the clerk of the Douglas School Board.

It was initially thought that John Lewin was on the *Ellan Vannin*. However, for some reason which has never been explained, he had crossed to Liverpool by an earlier sailing and therefore avoided certain death.

Mr Wright

The official number of passengers was fourteen. However there may have been a fifteenth: Mr Wright. What little is known about Mr Wright has come from Mrs Justine Dixon-Hughes, his great-granddaughter. Family tradition has it that he was travelling that night without a ticket. He lived somewhere in north-west England and had been visiting the Island on business. He was a cousin of Captain Teare who had agreed to give him a free trip back to Liverpool. Mr Wright was said to be a very mean man who would not pay for anything unless he had to.

However, despite this family story, the death of Mr Wright was never referred to in any newspaper or other report, and the death toll for passengers was officially finalised at fourteen.

No criticism could be made of the crewing arrangements on the *Ellan Vannin* for her trip from Ramsey to Liverpool on 3rd December 1909. As we shall see, there were three members of crew who were qualified to take command of the vessel.

There were 21 members of crew but only 14 passengers and there are various reasons why the crew outnumbered the passengers. Crew numbers are, to a certain extent, fixed, no matter how many passengers might be travelling. A minimum number of crew is needed to operate a vessel. For example, there must be a captain, an engineer, a fireman, a cook, a steward and so on. It should also be remembered that low passenger numbers were quite frequent in respect of winter crossings. This would apply particularly to a night crossing in December from Ramsey. Further, the Steam Packet tried to employ as many crew members as possible in the winter season and this too may account for the high ratio of crew to passengers. Those from other ships would be employed under special winter service conditions which provided some work between the busy summer seasons. However, this winter work was often at a lower rank.

There were eleven members of the crew from Douglas, three from Ramsey, five from various other parts of the Island and two from Liverpool.

Captain James Teare

It is inevitable that following any disaster rumours persist that have no relation to the established facts. Indeed, fifty years after the *Ellan Vannin* sank, a correspondent in the *Liverpool Express and Echo* of 22nd April 1959 maintained that the Captain's wife and twins were aboard and that the babies drowned in their bunks whilst asleep. This touching tale is not correct. The Captain's wife and

'One feels that it is something to be a Manx Captain, and that to be a Captain in the service of the Isle of Man Steam Packet Company is not far from a patent of nobility, I had almost said, by hereditary descent'

Revd T E Brown, the Manx poet.

Captain James Teare

children, none of whom were twins, received assistance from the Fund established for dependants of those lost, for many years after the disaster.

Captain James Teare lived in Palatine Road, Douglas. He was originally a Peel man and first took charge of a Steam Packet vessel in 1904 when he became captain of the *Ellan Vannin*. Before that, he had sailed in foreign waters for some years, and had risen from the position of an ordinary seaman to that of a captain. Lloyd's Register of captains' voyages records nothing against Captain Teare's name. This would suggest that he only sailed as a captain in the waters off the United Kingdom. In all probability he only captained Steam Packet vessels which would not have taken him outside of the Irish Sea. In other words, his certificate of competency to be a master was for home trade only.

In the summer of 1909 he had command of the *King Orry II*. The *King Orry* was an iron paddle steamer. She was, however, a much bigger and faster ship than the *Ellan Vannin,* having a gross tonnage, after alteration in 1888, of 1,104 tons and a maximum speed of 17 knots.

The title 'Captain' is a Royal Naval title. The person in charge of a merchant ship is a 'Master'. However, the title Captain is used to describe the

master of Steam Packet and other vessels because he is popularly described, albeit possibly incorrectly, as such.

As we have seen, Captain Teare was one of the most cautious of the Steam Packet's captains and was also felt to be one of its most capable captains. Crew members said of him that they had never been with a safer captain, because he was never away from his post. He was also described as one of nature's gentlemen. He was a lifelong teetotaller.

In 1909, as today, most of the Steam Packet's business was in the summer and it was a rule to give each of the Company's captains a month's winter work rather than dispense with their services until the following summer. It was on this basis that Captain Teare, because he knew the ship so well, joined the *Ellan Vannin* on Thursday 2nd December 1909, relieving Captain Cain who had just completed his month's winter service. As Daniel Defoe said, 'even the best of men cannot suspend their fate' and this, sadly, applied to Captain Teare.

He left a widow of 33 and four children: James (10), Douglas (8), Maggie (6) and Bertie (2). His wages had been £4 a week and his reported means were £200 (his house) and a £200 insurance policy. Captain Teare was one of those Steam Packet captains of whom it could truly be said the he was married to the Company. His wife was a daughter of the late William Cowley who had been chief officer of the *King Orry*. She was also a niece of Captain Cowley of the *Queen Victoria*.

Steam Packet Rules and Regulations

60. The Captain on taking charge of a Ship shall see that an Officer (or Coxswain) and Crew are appointed to each boat, and that every man is appointed to his place at Fire Station. Each Officer shall be responsible for the boat to which he is appointed being kept in good order and ready for immediate service. The boats shall be kept in such a condition of efficiency that they can be lowered without unneccessary delay (two boats being always kept ready for lowering.)

John Craine - First Mate

John Craine - First Mate

John Craine lived at Leigh Terrace, Douglas. He was aged about 44 and was first mate of the *Ellan Vannin*. The first mate was next in the line of command after the captain. He joined the Steam Packet in 1881 as a galley boy and later became a cook and afterwards he went into the forecastle. He then left the Company for a while but returned and entered the Steam Packet's employment as a sailor. A few years later he took his master's ticket. In the summer months he sailed as first mate on the *Mona III*.

Although John Craine was qualified to be a captain by virtue of his master's ticket, there is no record of him in Lloyd's Register of captains' voyages. Again, this would suggest that if he ever captained a vessel it would only have sailed in waters surrounding the United Kingdom. In his younger days Mr Craine was an enthusiastic rugby footballer, playing for both the Mona and Douglas clubs. His wages were 45 shillings a week in the summer, and 40 shillings in the winter.

He left a widow aged 42 and five children aged 17, 14, 13, 9 and 4. His widow was the daughter of Mr Teare, the Douglas to Peel carrier.

John Thomas Kinley - Second Mate

John Kinley lived at Surby, Port Erin. He was aged about 27 and was second mate on the *Ellan*

John Thomas Kinley - Second Mate

Vannin. A very promising young officer, he too was qualified to captain the vessel, holding a master seaman's certificate. During the summer he sailed as first mate on the *Fenella*. There is no record of him in Lloyd's Register of captains' voyages.

As one might expect of a young man in his position, he was very well known in Douglas and was a member of the Rocket Corps Ambulance Class. He had secured his first aid certificate in May 1909. He was said to have had wide experience as a sailor, particularly schooner sailing. He was unmarried and he left a father and mother who lived in the south of the Island.

Had he lived he may, in later years, have held a very senior position with the Steam Packet. He was the elder brother of Captain Albert Kinley, Marine Superintendent of the Company from 1933 to 1956. At the time of the disaster Albert Kinley was employed as a Steam Packet seaman and in later life his firmly expressed opinion was that the *Ellan Vannin* should never have sailed that night. He was also related to Captain Vernon Kinley, the late Deputy Marine Superintendent of the Steam Packet who died in 1998.

Edward Bellis - Chief Engineer

Edward Bellis, the chief or first engineer, was a Liverpool man. According to some accounts he lived at 43, Dyson Street, Walton, Liverpool. He had been

Edward Bellis - Chief Engineer

on the *Ellan Vannin* for four years, but little else is known of his Steam Packet service or his life generally. Indeed, such is the lack of information about him that some say he lived in Alexandra Road, Great Crosby, Lancashire. Certainly, the Alexandra Road address is that given in the Probate Registry. He was said to be popular among his shipmates. He left a widow and one child.

James Shepherd Cunningham - Carpenter

James Shepherd Cunningham - Carpenter

James Cunningham lived in Mona Terrace, Douglas. He was the *Ellan Vannin*'s carpenter. It should perhaps be mentioned that in 1909 much of the *Ellan Vannin*'s structure was wood and it was usual for a vessel to carry its own carpenter to undertake such repairs as were necessary in the course of a

voyage. Although today, many repairs are done when the vessel reaches port, Steam Packet passenger ships still have a carpenter as a member of the crew. Today's carpenter is very much more of a general maintenance man than someone who only works with wood.

James Cunningham came from Scotland and first worked on the Island when the Chicken Rock Lighthouse was being constructed. The Chicken Rock Lighthouse was built between 1869 and 1875, and when the work was finished he continued to live in Port St. Mary, working as a carpenter. He was reported by residents to be successful at his job, and at one time he owned a schooner and sailing craft.

He had married a Miss Hudson, a local girl, but after living in the town for some 20 years they moved to Douglas after which time he started to work for the Steam Packet. No details of his service with the Company are available.

Mr Cunningham left a widow and five daughters. His only son, who had been an engineer, died a couple of years before his father in tragic circumstances. He was shot by accident on his ship which was moored in the Manchester Ship Canal.

John William Cook - Able Seaman

John William Cook - Able Seaman

John Cook lived in Patrick Street, Peel, and was a native of that town. He was a 53 years old able seaman on the *Ellan Vannin*. No other details about his Steam Packet service are known. Whilst he was never a deep sea sailor he used to follow the fishing trade in the off-season when not employed by the Steam Packet.

He was a member of the Peel lifeboat crew and took part in the heroic rescue of 23 people from the *St. George* which went ashore near Peel Castle. In recognition of this remarkable rescue he was presented with a medal by the Norwegian Government. He left a widow and three children.

There are two postscripts concerning John Cook. Firstly, week in week out he went ashore when the *Ellan Vannin* was in Ramsey to collect a letter that would be waiting for him at the agent's office addressed to 'Mr John Cook c/o SS Ellan Vannin'. There was such a letter waiting for him on 2nd December 1909, but this time, for some reason, he did not collect it. The letter remained at the agent's office. Why he did not collect this particular letter and who the letters were from has never been explained.

The second postscript concerns a note in the *Isle of Man Examiner* of 4th December 1981 by his niece, Edith Chandler, of Peel. She wrote that her uncle was very proud of the *Ellan Vannin* and he would get upset when people joked that the *Ellan Vannin* could be put down the funnel of the *SS Lusitania* and could not be seen. Edith Chandler had other connections with the *Ellan Vannin* because another of her uncles (Harry Hough) had been a captain of the vessel and only ceased service when his eyesight failed and he was forced to retire.

John Cook's body was recovered from the shore at Blackpool in February 1910. His unopened pay-packet was found in his trousers; the name was still visible, having been written in indelible pencil. His niece was given a sixpence from the pay packet by her father. A Douglas jeweller engraved the three legs of Man in the centre and the date, 3 December 1909, was engraved around the rim. She wore this as a pendant for fifty years until she gave it to the Manx Museum where it is today.

John Benson - Seaman

John Benson lived at 14, King Street, Ramsey. He was about 54 years old and was employed as a

THE CREW

John Benson - Seaman

seaman on the *Ellan Vannin*. He had been employed by the Steam Packet for some 20 years and had served on most of the Company's vessels. In the winter, if he was not working for the Steam Packet, he usually worked on coasters or ships going to foreign countries.

He was a Ramsey man and was married to a daughter of Mr Samuel Cooper of Ramsey. He left a widow and four children: Willie (23), Annie (20), Maggie (16) and Bobby (12).

Thomas Corkish - Seaman

Thomas Corkish - Seaman

Thomas Corkish lived at 15 Church Street, Ramsey, and was employed as a seaman on the *Ellan Vannin*. He had various Ramsey connections,

including having been a member of the Ramsey lifeboat crew for many years. He had married the daughter of Mr William Taylor, who for a long time had supervised the Queen's Pier at Ramsey. Details of his Steam Packet service are not known. It is reported that in his early years he engaged in fishing in the winter months.

He left a widow and four children, the oldest being 17. Some accounts report that one of his children was an inmate of the Ramsey Cottage Hospital at the time of the disaster, but this was only for treatment for a deformed foot. Other reports stated that one child was at the Liverpool Infirmary for surgery. Over the course of time details become confused. It is possible that only one child was in hospital at the time the *Ellan Vannin* sank; the location of the hospital and reason for the admission differing according to who was asked.

William Kelly - Seaman

William Kelly - Seaman

William Kelly lived in Mill Street, Castletown, where his father worked at the gasworks. He held a first mate's certificate and in the summer he sailed as second mate on the *Tynwald III*.

A brother of Mr Kelly was due to take the *Ellan Vannin*'s sailing to Liverpool, having been on board for the whole of the summer. However, the brother became ill with influenza and Mr Kelly took his place. When the news of the tragedy reached his widow, Mrs Kelly was actually reading a letter from him. We can hardly imagine the horror of the circumstances that she and many other widows found themselves in. She was left to bring up six children, the eldest of whom was only 11 years old.

THE CREW

Mr Kelly had worked hard to qualify for his first mate's certificate and his widow always regretted giving the press a photograph which showed her husband not wearing his mate's uniform. The photograph above is of Mr Kelly in his mate's uniform. The author is grateful to Mr Kelly's granddaughter for enabling her grandmother's dying wish to be realised: recognition that although sailing as an ordinary seaman on the *Ellan Vannin*, Mr Kelly had his first mate's certificate.

Richard Alfred Clague - Seaman

Richard Alfred Clague - Seaman

Richard Clague lived at 1, Barrack Street, Douglas. He was engaged as a seaman on the *Ellan Vannin* but he may also have held an officer's certificate. He came from the south of the Island but for some twenty years had lived in Douglas. He suffered greatly from rheumatism and prior to joining the *Ellan Vannin*, a week before she sank, he was laid up on account of his rheumatics. It was said of him that despite his suffering he was always a genial and good-hearted man.

Steam Packet Rules and Regulations

100. The Chief Officer to be held responsible for the condition of the ship's boats and boat equipments, and whilst at sea all boats must be fully equipped and ready for lowering.

Although no other details of his Steam Packet service are known it is believed that he had been a long standing employee of the Company. He left a widow and five children.

James Lambert Crowley - Seaman

James Lambert Crowley - Seaman

James Crowley lived in Buck's Road, Douglas. Although James Crowley was only employed as a seaman on the *Ellan Vannin* he was another member of the crew who held a mate's certificate. He had sailed on the vessel in the summer of 1909 as second mate. Indeed, he had a long connection with the *Ellan Vannin*, having sailed on her as an ordinary seaman, as second mate and mate. He left a widow and eight children. From the very first printed reports his name was misspelt as Crawley, an error which persisted for many years and was perpetuated in the report of the Board of Trade Enquiry.

Servetus Rydings - Donkeyman

Servetus Rydings, or Samuel as he was popularly known, was employed as a donkeyman on the *Ellan Vannin* and lived in the 'Big House', South Quay, Douglas. He had served on the *Ellan Vannin* for several years. A donkeyman was a post held on steamers and he was expected to grease and oil the numerous moving parts of the ship's engines. He was also required to fire the 'donkey' boiler. This was an ancilliary power source, providing steam to run certain

Servetus Rydings - Donkeyman

machinery while the ship was in harbour and running the main boilers would have been too costly.

Little is known of Mr Rydings's personal circumstances, except that he was born in Heywood, Lancashire. Before living on the Island he was the licensee of the Cotton Tree Inn at Heywood. He left a widow and four children, one of whom, a 19 year old daughter, was an invalid.

Another of the numerous cases of premonition surrounding the sinking of the *Ellan Vannin* was reported many years later in connection with Servetus Rydings in the *Liverpool Express and Echo* of 22nd April 1959. A Mrs Travis, who used to live in Corinthian Street, Seaforth, near to the shore of the River Mersey, woke her husband on the morning of 3rd December 1909 at about 3.00am. Although Mrs Travis was deaf, she said she could hear terrible screams from a ship that was in distress. Early the next day she spoke to her next door neighbour who was in fact the sister-in-law of Rydings, and she claimed to have seen him at the top of the stairs the previous night. The conversation between these neighbours, both of whom had suffered premonitions of what was to come, took place at a time when they could not have known of the disaster. News of the sinking of the *Ellan Vannin* would not have been known in Liverpool until later that day.

Fred Craine - Second Engineer

Fred Craine lived in Wynton Villa, Laureston Road, Douglas, and was the second engineer on the *Ellan Vannin*. He was aged about 27. He was a member of the Buck's Road Primitive Methodist

Fred Craine - Second Engineer

Church. He left a widow, a daughter of Mr W H Cubbon, who was a grocer in Victoria Road, Douglas, and one child.

Walter Cannell - Fireman

Walter Cannell - Fireman

Walter Cannell lived at 4, Dukes Road, Douglas and was employed as a fireman on the *Ellan Vannin*. A fireman's main duties were to put fuel on the fire to keep the boilers in steam and to remove the ash, which would be put over the side of the vessel. Traditionally, one of the fireman would act as the 'spareman'. The spareman relieved others but also had the duty of looking after the engineering officers' rooms as they had no stewards. It is not known if this practice operated on the *Ellan Vannin*. Mr Cannell's brother was also employed by the Steam Packet as a fireman on the *Douglas III*, but little else is known of his employment with the Steam Packet or his personal circumstances. He was a married man and left a widow, but no children.

John Clegg Taubman - Fireman

John Clegg Taubman - Fireman

John Taubman lived at Big Well Street, Douglas, and was aged about 25 years. He was a fireman on the *Ellan Vannin* but no other details about his service are known. Some reports say his father worked for the Douglas Gaslight Company, whereas others say his father was a stonemason. He himself was a member of the Douglas Club. He had been a prominent rugby football player. He also had done service in the army, but left after a few years and returned to the Island taking up a position with the Steam Packet. Mr Taubman left a widow and two children.

William J Shimmin

William J Shimmin

William Shimmin lived at 11, Waterloo Road, Ramsey, nearly opposite the Wesleyan Chapel. Mr

Shimmin was described in some reports as a fireman on the *Ellan Vannin*, whereas other reports describe him as being a donkeyman. Apart from this uncertainty about his job there are no other details known about his service, either on the *Ellan Vannin* or on other of the Steam Packet's vessels. He left a widow, who was in poor health, and four children, one of whom was born after the disaster.

Joseph Crellin - Fireman

Joseph Crellin - Fireman

Joseph Crellin lived in a cottage at Glen Vine, Crosby. He was a fireman on the *Ellan Vannin*, a position he had held for some years. Nothing else is known about his service with the Company. He had lived at Glen Vine for many years with his family and was closely involved with the Wesleyan Methodist Church in Crosby, where he was a teacher in the Sunday school. He was a staunch teetotaller and a member of the Good Samaritan Rechabite Tent. He left a widow, who originally came from Ballamodda, and three sons who were all aged under ten.

Thomas Stubbs - Chief Steward

Mr Stubbs came from Liverpool. He was chief steward on the *Ellan Vannin* and had served for approximately 20 years on Steam Packet ships. Although he was a Liverpool man he had many friends and acquaintances on the Island. He left a widow and six children. One of the stewards (Mr Fogerty) had been suspended prior to sailing and an

immediate replacement was needed, and it seems possible that Mr Stubbs was the replacement as he was regularly the chief steward on the *Ellan Vannin*. If he did replace the suspended chief steward and thereby loose his life, it is perhaps surprising that his family made no mention of this fact later.

Herbert Holden Holland - Second Steward

Herbert Holden Holland - Second Steward

Herbert (Bert) Holland lived on Head Road, Douglas. He was second steward on the *Ellan Vannin* but no other details about his Steam Packet service are known. Reports after the disaster claimed that he had joined the ship at the last moment, and it could be that he was the replacement for Mr Shipsides whose premonition had made him sign off the vessel a short while before. Mr Holland probably came from Onchan as his mother lived at Alpine Terrace in Onchan. He was described as a most courteous and obliging steward. He left a widow, who was the daughter of Mr Alex Lewthwaite, stationer and book-binder of Market Hill, Douglas, and one child.

Mrs Eliza Collister - Stewardess

Mrs Collister lived at Glen Vine, Crosby. She was the stewardess on the *Ellan Vannin* and would have been responsible for the female passengers.

She was aged about 40 and the widow of the late Mr Louis Collister, of East Foxdale who had died eight years previously. She and her husband had lived in America and South Africa where he was a miner, but failing health

Mrs Eliza Collister - Stewardess

had forced her husband to return to the Island. They had lost heavily in the Dumbell's Bank crash of 1900. She had lived in Glen Vine, Crosby, before she married but in 1909 she was running a boarding house in Farrant Street in Douglas during the summer and working with the Steam Packet during the winter. There are no other details about her Packet service except that she was said to be very popular with the passengers because of her kindly manner. This approach was much appreciated especially on rough crossings. She left a nine year old daughter.

Edward Burke - Cook

Edward Burke lived in Derby Road, Douglas. He was 65 years old and the *Ellan Vannin*'s cook. He would only be cook for the passengers. In the *Ellan Vannin*'s days the crew would provide and prepare their own food. Wives and girlfriends bringing baskets of food was a familiar sight when a ship was in harbour. It was not until the 1960s that the Steam Packet provided the food and a cook to prepare meals for the crew.

Rather unusually for 1909, Mr Burke had been divorced. By his first wife he left a son and a daughter. His son worked on the Steam Packet's *Tynwald III* where it seems his daughter was a cook. His first wife had not been in good health and was awaiting an operation when the *Ellan Vannin* sank. His second wife was a professional lady, being a nurse and midwife. As far as is known there were no children by his second marriage. There are no other recorded details of Mr Burke's Steam Packet service.

THE CREW

SUPPLEMENT TO "THE ISLE OF MAN WEEKLY TIMES" OF SATURDAY, DECEMBER 11, 1909.

WRECK OF THE ELLAN VANNIN

Mrs. HEATON JOHNSON (Passenger).

J. CUNNINGHAM (Carpenter).

Captain JAMES TEARE.

F. CRAINE (2nd Engineer).

HEATON JOHNSON (Passenger).

MARK H. JOUGHIN (Passenger).

Mrs CRIX (Passenger).

WM. KELLY (Seaman).

BERT HOLLAND (Steward).

W. CANNELL (Fireman).

S. RYDINGS (Donkeyman).

J. CRELLIN (Fireman).

W. SHIMMIN (Donkeyman).

A. CLAGUE (Seaman).

THOS. QUAYLE (Passenger).

THE ELLAN VANNIN
ENTERING RAMSEY HARBOUR.

Built as a Paddle Steamer by Tod & McGregor, Glasgow, in the year 1860. Lengthened and converted into a Twin Screw in the year 1883.
FOUNDERED AT THE MERSEY BAR, FRIDAY, DECEMBER 3rd, 1909, AND ALL ON BOARD LOST.

J. CRAWLEY (Seaman).

E. GELLISS (1st Engineer).

J. KINLEY (2nd Mate).

W. E. HIGGINBOTHAM (Passenger).

Mrs COLLISTER (Stewardess).

Miss FISHER (Passenger).

J. BENSON (Seaman).

E. J. BLEVIN (Passenger).

T. CORKISH (Seaman).

J. COOKE (Seaman).

T. TAUBMAN (Fireman).

J. CRAINE (1st Mate).

Brown & Sons, Ltd., Printers, Douglas, Isle of Man.

THIS POSTER, SHOWING THE MAJORITY OF THE PASSENGERS AND CREW LOST ON THE ELLAN VANNIN, WAS PRODUCED BY THE ISLE OF MAN WEEKLY TIMES JUST ONE WEEK AFTER THE DISASTER. MANY MANX HOUSEHOLDS STILL HAVE A COPY OF THIS POSTER TODAY.

CHAPTER SIX

THE FIRST NEWS OF THE DISASTER

The *Ellan Vannin* was due at Salisbury Dock in Liverpool at around 8.00am on 3rd December. These were days when ships travelled much more in the hope rather than the expectation of arriving at a particular time. Arrival times were very approximate.

Probably because of the night's storms someone at the Steam Packet's head office in Douglas telegraphed the Company's Ramsey agent, Mr Bell, at 9.45am. The telegram simply asked 'Did the Vannin sail at 1.00am this morning?'

At Liverpool, responsibility for discharging the cargo and passengers from the *Ellan Vannin* rested with the Company's long serving agents, Thomas Orford & Sons. The agents must have been used to late arrivals from the Island. We can assume that because of the very bad weather and the fact that the *Ellan Vannin* was one of the Company's slowest ships, the agents would not have been unduly concerned by the ship's late arrival on this December morning. However, the agents did telegraph Mr Bell at 11.45am. Their telegram showed no concern, merely informing Mr Bell that there was, as yet, no sign of the *Ellan Vannin*.

Meanwhile, back on the Island, some of Ramsey's residents, having suffered a dreadful night of gales, began to wonder if the *Ellan Vannin* had arrived safely in Liverpool. A number of telegrams were sent to Liverpool at about 11.00am. The replies received shortly afterwards were all to the same effect: there was no news, the *Ellan Vannin* had not yet arrived.

The regular Douglas and Liverpool Steam Packet ferries were unable to provide any explanation for the missing *Ellan Vannin*. The *Fenella*, which had sailed across from Liverpool the night before through the storm, departed from Douglas back to Liverpool at 9.00am. The *Douglas* departed from Liverpool for Douglas at 11.30am. Neither vessel saw any sign of the *Ellan Vannin*.

The agents did however contact Fleetwood, a port some miles to the north of Liverpool, to see if the *Ellan Vannin* had put in there, either as a result of being damaged or for shelter. The agents also checked to confirm that the *Ellan Vannin* had not turned back to Ramsey or sheltered in Douglas. By early afternoon the agents may have been wondering if misfortune had befallen the *Ellan Vannin*. However, the first real indication of the calamity that had occurred was a request, sometime in the afternoon of 3rd December, for the agents to visit the Mersey Docks and Harbour Board's Marine Surveyor.

The request came after a report from the Formby Lightship. At 12.30pm the crew of the lightship had picked up a mail hamper and two lifebuoys from the Crosby Channel near Taylor's Bank. Other items were also recovered. The lifebuoys had on them the name *Ellan Vannin*. Orford & Sons

THE TELEGRAM SENT FROM THE STEAM PACKET'S LIVERPOOL AGENTS TO THE RAMSEY AGENT ON THE MORNING OF 3RD DECEMBER.
'STEAMERS RAMSEY' WAS THE TELEGRAPHIC ADDRESS OF THE COMPANY'S RAMSEY OFFICE.

'You gentlemen of England
who live at home at ease
How little do you think
of the dangers of the seas'

From the 'Valiant Sailors'.

THE FIRST NEWS OF THE DISASTER

**THOMAS ORFORD, THE FOUNDER OF THE
COMPANY THAT WAS THE STEAM PACKET'S
LIVERPOOL AGENTS, AND HIS SON JOSEPH, WHO
WAS THE AGENT AT THE TIME OF THE DISASTER.**

were asked to visit the Marine Surveyor's offices, to where the various items had been brought. The significance of these finds was immediately appreciated by the agents. The mail hamper was taken to Birkenhead post office, and at 5.00pm the agents telegraphed the Company's head office. The telegram from Orford & Sons conveyed the worst possible news:

> '... have just returned from Marine Surveyor. Basket of mail, two lifebuoys marked *Ellan Vannin*, bags of turnips, a piano, sofa cushions, found floating past Formby Lightship today.
>
> The Post Office advised to send to Woodside for the mail. We fear a serious calamity.'

Down at the harbour in Ramsey people had been calling into the Company's agent's office throughout the afternoon to make enquiries about the *Ellan Vannin*'s arrival. Mr Bell had given hopeful

answers. But when, at about 6.00pm, he had to tell them of the telegram received in Douglas, his office was besieged. The gloom on everyone's faces, as they milled around the East Quay, told what all were dreading: the *Ellan Vannin* was lost.

Orford & Sons' fears were understandable. It was unlikely that these items had been washed overboard in the storm, but it was still possible that the *Ellan Vannin* was afloat, having been either disabled by the storm or found shelter. For a brief period it was rumoured that the *Ellan Vannin* was in the Fleetwood area. Following receipt of the telegram William Corkhill, the Steam Packet's General Manager, summoned the directors to an emergency board meeting. It was a markedly different atmosphere from the board meeting the day before when the directors had been considering the details for the christening ceremony of the Company's new ship, *Snaefell III*.

Not all of the board could attend the emergency meeting. The chair was taken by Mr Maitland. Messrs Waid and Hughes-Games were the other directors present. The contents of the telegram were read to the directors by Mr Corkhill. A further telegram from Orford & Sons was received at 7.00pm. This telegram compounded the fears that the vessel was lost. The mail basket recovered earlier had been opened and found to contain mail from Ramsey. The mail could only have come from the *Ellan Vannin*.

The contents of the 7.00pm telegram were immediately communicated to the Company's agent in Ramsey. The throng of people now surging around his office received in despair his solemn repetition of this latest information from Douglas. Less than 24 hours before, the *Ellan Vannin* had left Ramsey for a routine voyage to Liverpool. Now fathers, sons, mothers, daughters, brothers and sisters all appeared lost.

The board waited anxiously for further news. Shortly before 10.00pm Orford & Sons telegraphed that there was nothing further to report except that the wet weather was continuing. When the directors ended their meeting there was still no conclusive evidence that the *Ellan Vannin* had sunk, however, some action was obviously required and the Commodore of the fleet, Captain Keig, was instructed to go to Liverpool on the morning boat (4th December). Captain Keig's

mission was to try and obtain fuller particulars of the fate of the *Ellan Vannin*.

The non-arrival of the *Ellan Vannin* was headline news the next day not just on the Island but in England as well. The *Manchester Guardian* attached particular significance to the recovery of the mail. The reporter felt that finding dead sheep, turnips, lifebelts and lifebuoys alone might have meant that these had been swept from the deck but that the ship itself was still safe, but the finding of the mail, assumed to have been stored below, must have meant that the ship had sunk.

The directors were in sombre mood as they assembled at 10.00am on 4th December in the boardroom at the Steam Packet's Douglas headquarters. The three directors who had met until 10.00pm the night before were joined by Messrs Elliott and Kitto, the remaining members of the board. There had been no significant developments overnight. The directors remained in session throughout the day.

In the course of the morning further messages were received. At about 10.30am Orford & Sons advised by telegram that one of *Ellan Vannin*'s lifeboats and part of the bridge had been washed ashore on the banks of the River Mersey at New Brighton. The lifeboat was found bumping gently against the sandstone rocks at the foot of the New Brighton lighthouse. The number '1' on its bow showed that it had been the lifeboat on the starboard side. When found, the boat was covered with her canvas. Not a lash of the canvas had been disturbed. There was evidence that she had been torn from her holding place: the starboard gunwale at the two points where the wooden grips would hold her in position was broken. Some great force had wrenched the lifeboat from her fastenings and she had floated free when the *Ellan Vannin* sank. Her mast and oars lay neatly lashed inside, her water-cask, too, and her rudder, were all ready for shipping. The most significant damage to the section of bridge that was found was that one of its white painted handrails was bent as though by some great wrench.

Saturday morning's tide had brought more

evidence of disaster. The water was thickly dotted with wreckage. One report described many planks floating in the water along with a lifebelt, part of a ship's boat and many thin boards. Most significant of all—a mahogany tumbler-rack was in the water. The rack was a saloon fitting. Any damage to a ship that breaks up its saloon is going to threaten the ship's ability to stay afloat.

But although over 24 hours overdue there was still no definite news that the *Ellan Vannin* had sunk. Various ports were contacted to see if the ship had put into or sought shelter elsewhere. These contacts must have been made more in hope than expectation as the news of more wreckage being found continued to come in from Orford & Sons. However, optimists told of the occasions when the *Ellan Vannin* had taken as long as 27 hours to reach Liverpool.

Finally, at 4.00pm on 4th December, the fears became reality. A telegram from Orford & Sons reported the grim news that the wreck of the *Ellan Vannin* had been found. The telegram gave the position of the wreck as 200 yards south-south west, half a mile west of the Q1 black can gas buoy. In other words, the wreck was situated between the Bar Lightship and the outer buoy, the Q1, on the port (left) side at the start of the channel to the docks in Liverpool, and approximately 14 miles from the Liverpool landing stage. She was lying in about 30 feet of water at low tide.

The position of the wreck on the then current Admiralty chart lay on the absolutely straight line between the Bar and Formby lightships. It would seem the ship was on a true course. She was about two thirds of a mile from the Bar Lightship and 3 miles from the Formby Lightship. She lay in the outermost part of the channel but would seem not to have entered between the banks which were left and right, inward from the line of buoys.

Where the *Ellan Vannin* sank was very much at the 'gut' or narrowest part of the entrance to the channel. The tide coming out and meeting the winds from the opposite direction would have made the seas very treacherous.

Although it is not recorded in the beautiful

Special Meeting

"Ellan Vannin"

Douglas
3rd December 1909
Friday.

Present

Mr Maitland Chairman
" Waid
" Hughes-Games

Meeting called on receipt of the following telegram from Lpool agents, to hand at 5.30 p.m.

"No account of 'Ellan Vannin'. Just returned from marine surveyor who reports that basket mails, two lifebuoys marked 'Ellan Vannin' bags of turnips, and a piano and some plush sofa cushions were observed floating past Formby lightship at 12.30 p.m. today. Piano and mail hamper picked up. Post office advised to send to Woodside for it. Will advise later any further particulars gathered. We fear serious calamity".

It had blown with hurricane force from North West in the early hours of the morning after the Vannin had left Ramsey at 1 a.m. and the above were was the first definite news information in reply to telegraph enquiries throughout the day as to the whereabouts of the steamer. A further message despatched from Liverpool at 7 p.m. advised that the hamper of mails picked up is from Ramsey and that certain carcases of sheep were seen floating in the channel (the Vannin's deck cargo consisted of 88 sheep and 1 pig) but so far as could be ascertained nothing had been seen of the Vannin by the light ships, or by any inward bound steamer.

The Board sat until 1.0 p.m. and shortly before that hour Oxfords telegraphed:— Nothing further to report, weather wet with heavy squalls at intervals".

Vettartland. Chairman

THE MINUTES OF THE STEAM PACKET'S EMERGENCY BOARD MEETING ON THE EVENING OF 3RD DECEMBER 1909.

THE ELLAN VANNIN STORY

copper plate hand-written minutes of the board meeting, it is highly probable that they had to consider which ship would be used as the *Ellan Vannin*'s immediate replacement. On the Friday evening the crew of the *Tynwald III* were instructed to report to Liverpool for the next morning as the *Tynwald* was to go on the Liverpool/Douglas route. The *Tynwald* would replace the *Fenella* which was instructed to carry out the *Ellan Vannin*'s duties. The meeting was adjourned until a special board meeting on Monday 6th December.

In 1909 there were five newspapers published in the Isle of Man. Many published special editions to keep the public fully up to date with news of the *Ellan Vannin*. Thousands of copies were quickly bought. The headlines in Saturday's newspapers eloquently described what everyone was feeling. The *Isle of Man Weekly Times* was typical, 'Feared loss of the Ellan Vannin'. In Ramsey people crowded around the offices of the *Ramsey Courier and Northern Advertiser* waiting for the next special edition.

The people of the Isle of Man were, as Island races everywhere, well used to disasters at sea. Over a hundred years before, at the end of the eighteenth century, nearly 200 men died when a sudden storm hit the Manx herring fleet at Douglas. In the 1860s the magnificent Liverpool ship the *James Crossfield* ran ashore at Langness in the south of the Island drowning everyone aboard. Towards the end of the nineteenth century the Norwegian barque, *Nelson Rice*, was swept onto the rocks a few miles south of Douglas at Port Soderick. The crew of 12 were killed.

The boats of the herring fleet were small boats, the *James Crossfield* and *Nelson Rice* were not Manx ships and the reasons for their loss could easily be understood. What stunned all the population was not just that the *Ellan Vannin* was a Manx ship with Manx passengers and crew, but that its disappearance was so sudden and inexplicable. Only those Islanders over 50 would have known of times when the *Ellan Vannin* was not an integral part of the Steam Packet's fleet. She was a landmark in the Company's history. The sinking of the *Ellan Vannin* was like the loss of an old and trusted friend.

As the special editions of the newspapers carried further details of the non-arrival of the *Ellan Vannin* in Liverpool the real possibility of her loss brought such headlines as 'A Nation in Mourning'. This was indeed the case when any last lingering hopes that the *Ellan Vannin* was somehow safe were dashed on Saturday afternoon as special editions of the newspapers reported the stark reality that the wreck had been found.

The Mersey Docks and Harbour Board's Marine Surveyor, Lieutenant Mace and his assistant accompanied by divers, went to examine the Q1 buoy on board the Harbour Board's salvage steamer, *Salvor*. The buoy had been reported adrift. Attached to it was a quantity of wreckage. Nearby was the sunken *Ellan Vannin*. At low water one of the ship's masts was above sea level. A watch vessel was therefore placed close by to warn vessels of the danger of colliding with the wreckage.

The *Courier* received the news that the vessel had been located early on Saturday afternoon. The paper's special correspondent sent a telegram advising his newspaper that the *Ellan Vannin* had been found lying at the bottom of the channel near the Mersey Bar. The *Courier* put a notice to this effect in its window in Parliament Street, Ramsey. The exact location of the wreck was 1,170 yards from the Bar Lightship, and 1,000 yards from the position of the Q1 buoy on a direct line between them and broadside on to the tide.

Pathetic and unparalleled scenes were witnessed in Ramsey as the worst fears were realised. The *Courier*'s offices were surrounded by anxious people and a special edition was eagerly snapped up with copies being snatched from the printing presses. Women who had lost their husbands, children their fathers and others who had lost their friends and relatives were devastated. All were appalled by the tragic end of the *Ellan Vannin* just 36 hours before. Many remained up late into Saturday night weeping and mourning.

A December Sunday in Ramsey was usually a day of relaxation and worship. But not Sunday 5th December 1909. Church and other social activities were cancelled. It is said that literally thousands congregated in front of the *Courier's* offices which

remained open all day. People had come from Ramsey itself and from all over the Island. Everyone remained in despair as the news continued to come in that still no bodies had been recovered. There were similar scenes of grief in other parts of the Island and in Liverpool.

The Mersey Docks and Harbour Board's divers worked on Sunday 5th and Monday 6th December, exploring the sunken vessel and trying to recover the bodies of the passengers and crew. Their work was impeded by the muddy waters. Even with powerful electric lamps the divers could not see far. The shifting sands at the bottom of the channel and the fact that the *Ellan Vannin* was buried up to deck level in some places added to the divers' difficulties. Their work was restricted to a few hours a day at the turn of the tide.

However, the divers stuck to their task and were eventually able to provide the first indication of the circumstances in which the *Ellan Vannin* had sunk.

These first indications are of crucial importance in trying to understand the mysteries of the sinking of the *Ellan Vannin* because at the subsequent Board of Trade enquiry, the evidence heard from these divers differed dramatically from these early reports.

The divers' findings were described in a Steam Packet statement issued on Monday 6th December which advised that the *Ellan Vannin* had been sunk after a collision with an unknown vessel. One diver had found on the port side of the *Ellan Vannin* that from the chain locker towards the middle of the ship, her plates were smashed in for a distance of 14 feet. The edges of the plates were indented with a blow which suggested the *Ellan Vannin* had sunk after a collision. Another diver described the same findings but in a different way; he discovered a 14 foot hole between the forecastle head and the bridge. However the divers' findings were described, such damage, the divers concluded, could only have been caused by an impact with a heavy vessel. The directors of the Steam Packet were also convinced Captain Teare was on a navigable course at the time the ship was sunk. The statement they issued also expressed the firmly held opinion that no living sailor could have made a better passage.

The *Ellan Vannin* was in an upright position but in two parts. She had been severed about amidships and there was a distance of 15 to 25 feet between the parts. The divers also found that the davits on the starboard side had been swung out. The davits hold the lifeboats and finding them swung out suggested an attempt had been made to launch the starboard lifeboat, the one

---

No. 1930—*H.H.* W.*

ENGLAND, WEST COAST—LIVERPOOL BAY.

Queens channel entrance—Wreck.

Subject.—A wreck of the undermentioned description lies sunk in the entrance to Queens channel.

Position.—At a distance of about 5⅗₀ cables, S. 70° E., from the Bar light-vessel.

Lat. 53° 31¾′ N., long 3° 17′ W.

Description.—wreck of the s.s. Ellan Vannin.

Remarks.—A watch-vessel has been moored on the seaward side of the wreck.

Vessels should give this watch-vessel a wide berth.

Variation.—18° W.

(Notice No. 1930 *of* 1909.*)*

Charts temporarily affected.—No. 1951, Liverpool bay.

,, 1170*b*, Great Ormes head to Liverpool.

Publication.—West Coast of England, 1902, page 364.

Authority.—Mersey Docks and Harbour Board Notice, 6th December 1909.

A NOTICE OF CHANGE TO THE ADMIRALTY CHART WHICH SHOWS THE STEPS TAKEN TO WARN SHIPPING ABOUT THE WRECK OF THE ELLAN VANNIN.

that had been found floating at New Brighton. Interestingly, the other lifeboat was not found, and there remained for sometime the slight possibility that it may have been successfully launched. This would mean that some passengers and crew may have got away and could possibly still be alive.

The divers' view was that on the ships colliding the passengers and crew rushed to the deck hoping to get away in the lifeboats. However, before they could get away they were swept from the deck and drowned in the tempestuous seas. If this happened, their bodies would have been carried away by the outgoing tide. Support for this initial view came from the fact that the divers had not, at this stage, been able to find any bodies on the sunken *Ellan Vannin*.

What had happened to the unknown ship that had sunk *Ellan Vannin*? A number of possibilities were considered by the authorities. Had the unknown ship also sunk? A check of vessels revealed that none were unaccounted for. Therefore the conclusion was that some unknown ship, having sunk the *Ellan Vannin,* went on its way perhaps not even knowing of the collision. Apparently a number of liners were in the Mersey at the time of the disaster. Checks were put in hand to see if any ship arriving at or departing from Liverpool at the relevant time was the offending vessel. The enquiries revealed no evidence of a collision.

By this time there had been an opportunity for the Company to undertake a detailed study of what the divers had found. While there were many other theories as to the cause of the disaster, the Steam Packet's view was unambiguous. A statement was issued from the Company at 3.00pm on Tuesday 7th December. The Company's considered opinion was that the *Ellan Vannin* foundered after being in collision with a large steamer whose identity was, at present, unknown.

Unfortunately, the original report of the divers does not appear to have survived. The most detailed account appears in *The Times* of 10th December 1909. The damage is described in these terms:

'The fractured plating on the port bow was turned inwards. The edges of the plates on the port side are indented apparently by a blow. The fracture on the port side was 14 feet across

the top and extended in a V shape to the keel, which was broken. The starboard bow was also fractured. The collision hole on the port side was in the chain locker and the fore side of No. 2 bulkhead. This bulkhead was broken and the steerage was open to the sea.'

This report contains more detail than is in the Steam Packet's statement issued a few days previously. The conclusion to be drawn from those findings was however the same: the *Ellan Vannin* had sunk as the result of a collision.

The Marine Intelligence section of Lloyd's List, a daily bible for those involved in maritime matters, added support to the collision theory. The December 7th entry refers to the divers finding conclusive proof of a collision.

The divers' grim work of trying to bring the bodies of the deceased passengers and crew to the surface continued. The fact that the divers' early efforts to find the bodies were unsuccessful led to the false hope that somehow the passengers and crew were safe. A cruel rumour swept the Island that the *Ellan Vannin* had been in a collision with a Norwegian barque. The outward bound barque had not been badly damaged and had picked up all the passengers and crew. The barque had then landed the survivors in southern Ireland on the following Tuesday morning. This rumour led to fruitless enquiries being made.

Another cruel blow was the result of an incorrect press agency report. Many English papers reported that nine bodies from the *Ellan Vannin* had been found on Sunday 5th December. In fact, the bodies that had been recovered came from another ship. The press agency had muddled up the *Ellan Vannin* with the *Thistlemor* which had sunk hundreds of miles from Liverpool.

The divers were reluctant to enter the *Ellan Vannin*'s saloon where it was thought the bodies may be; they feared entangling their lifelines in the passages and stairs on their way to the saloon. The poor visibility due to the swirling sand also made them fear they wouldn't be able to find their way out of the ship. In an effort to placate the growing anxiety of the families the Steam Packet Commodore, Captain Keig,

went to encourage the divers in their efforts to find the bodies.

Any lingering doubts that there were any survivors were dashed when the first bodies were recovered from the wreck. On Thursday 9th December the divers recovered the body of one of the passengers, Ernest Allen. On the same day the body of one of the crew, the cook, Edward Burke was found floating in the ship's saloon. Press reports that the divers had recovered the body of another crewman, the second steward Herbert Holland, were incorrect.

The body of another crewman, John Taubman who was one of the firemen, was recovered on 13th December and his was the last to be recovered from the wreck. The top of the ship's saloon was smashed in and it is possible that the bodies of many of the passengers and crew floated out to the open sea. Of the 35 people lost only three bodies so far had been recovered. It was to be another five weeks before further bodies were found washed up on the shores of the River Mersey and the adjoining coasts.

Messages of sympathy came in from people in all walks of life. The Lieutenant Governor, Lord Raglan and his wife expressed their deepest sympathy and the Dowager Lady Loch, wife of a former Governor, sent a message as did the Bishop of Newcastle, formerly the Bishop of Sodor and Man.

Holidaymakers from Lancashire and Cheshire wrote to the newspapers, many comparing the fate of those lost with those who had holidayed on the Island but returned safely home.

The congregations at churches and chapels throughout the Island and elsewhere heard moving pulpit references. Prayers were offered for the widows and children. The Reverend Devall of St. Paul's Church, Ramsey, who had decided not to travel because of the weather, visited the homes of those who had lost someone in the disaster.

Details of all the services were reported in the newspapers. Perhaps the most moving was conducted by the Reverend J E Phillipson at the Primitive Church in Ramsey. He preached from the words 'It is good for us to draw nigh to God' and said:

'But death has come tragically and unexpectedly - in a way unparalleled in the history of our little town - and has cast its gloom upon us all. Strong brave men, tender-hearted women, and even a little child have without any warning been called from time to eternity. The terrible disaster in the Mersey on Friday last has caused our hearts to ache with sorrow, and our eyes to melt with tears. Our sincere sympathy goes out to those whose hearts and homes are left desolate. How the recent accident happened - that sorrow may never be told; one thing is sure, that the great heart of God is moved with compassion at the sorrow of those who are left behind. It is good for us to draw near to God in this time of trouble, for when we do so His light will shine upon our darkness; His comfort will soothe our sorrows; and a hope blooming with immortality will be ours.'

The service ended with the playing of the 'Dead March'.

The Lieutenant Governor decided a Fund should be opened for the relief of the dependants. Subscription lists were started

ONE OF THE MESSAGES OF SYMPATHY RECEIVED AT THE STEAM PACKET'S OFFICES. THIS ONE WAS FROM THE ISLAND'S BISHOP.

throughout the Island and elsewhere in the world.

A public meeting was held in Douglas. The Bishop of Sodor and Man presided as those attending discussed how to help the dependants. The Lieutenant Governor became President of the Fund's Committee and Mr R D Gelling, the Clerk of Tynwald, acted as Honorary Secretary.

Subscriptions could be made to the Isle of Man Bank, Parr's Bank, Lloyds Bank and the Lancashire & Yorkshire Bank. The Town Hall at Douglas and the offices of the Commissioners of Ramsey, Castletown, Peel, Port Erin, Port St. Mary and Laxey were also able to receive subscriptions as were any offices of the Island's newspapers. In England, the Company's Liverpool agents received subscriptions from those in the north-west and the Mayor of Liverpool started a Liverpool fund.

The Manx Electric Railway made the Ramsey Palace available for entertainments to be held in order to raise monies for the Fund.

There was a special board meeting of the Steam Packet directors on Monday 6th December. In addition to the directors a Mr J M Cruickshank was present as legal advisor. The advice to the board was that the Company's position would not be prejudiced by a contribution of £1,000 to the Fund. Such a speedy response of so large a contribution may explain, in part, why the Steam Packet has a place in the hearts and minds of all involved with the Isle of Man. The 2009 equivalent of £1,000 is just over £70,000. Of immediate practical help to the widows of the crew, the Steam Packet agreed to pay the crew's weekly wages to the widows until the Fund was operating. Such a benevolent approach to its employees might be compared with the crew of the *Titanic*. When the *Titanic* sank the crew were paid only until the time of the sinking.

In England, the Chairman of the Shipwrecked Fishermen and Mariners Royal Benevolent Society announced that, by 10th December, less than a week after the disaster, assistance had already been provided. Over £75 had been paid to widows of the crew in order to relieve immediate needs.

THE FIRST NEWS OF THE DISASTER

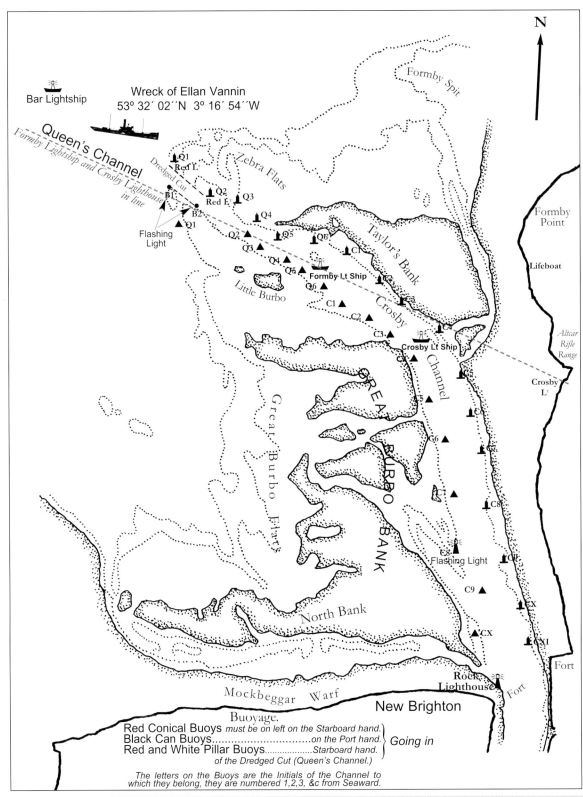

Bar Lightship

Wreck of Ellan Vannin
53° 32′ 02″N 3° 16′ 54″W

Queen's Channel

Formby Lightship and Crosby Lighthouse in line

Dredged Cut

Q1
Red L'

B1

Red E

Q2

Q3

B2

Q1

Flashing
Light

Q2

Zebra Flats

Q4

Q5

Q6

C'

Q3

Q4

Q5

Little Burbo

Q6

Formby Lt Ship

C1

C2

C3

Taylor's Bank

C'

C2

Crosby Channel

Crosby Lt Ship

C'

Great Burbo Flats

C5

C6

G6

C7

C8
Flashing Light

C9

Formby Spit

Formby Point

Lifeboat

Altcar Rifle Range

Crosby L'

CX

CX

CX1

GREAT BURBO BANK

North Bank

CX1

Rock
Lighthouse

Fort

Mockbeggar Warf

New Brighton

Fort

Buoyage.
Red Conical Buoys *must be on left on the Starboard hand.*
Black Can Buoys...............................*on the Port hand.* } *Going in*
Red and White Pillar Buoys..................*Starboard hand.*
of the Dredged Cut (Queen's Channel.)

*The letters on the Buoys are the Initials of the Channel to
which they belong, they are numbered 1,2,3, &c from Seaward.*

SITE OF THE WRECK OF THE ELLAN VANNIN TAKEN FROM A CONTEMPORARY CHART.

THE ELLAN VANNIN STORY

THE AFTERMATH OF THE DISASTER

Although grief and despair had not lifted there were, as after any disaster, practical matters to attend to.

The Mersey Docks and Harbour Board wished to blow up the wreck to avoid any danger to shipping and there was also the matter of settling the claims from those who had lost a relative or cargo. In the event, very few bodies were finally recovered. Out of a total of 35 passengers and crew, only 17 bodies were ever found. Three were recovered from the wreck by the divers and the other 14 were recovered from the neighbouring shores. The farthest point from where a body was recovered was at Blackpool, when on 16th February 1910 the body of John Cook was found. Blackpool is about 25 miles from where the ship sank.

The grizzly process of identifying decomposed bodies was punctuated by many false alarms. Many bodies that were at first assumed to be from the *Ellan Vannin* turned out to be from other tragedies altogether. Identification of the bodies was by similar means to those used today, as in many cases the prolonged exposure to the sea had made identification extremely difficult. Was there a pen, watch or glasses that would help? Various identifying items were more common in 1909 than they are today. For example, the records show that a number of bodies were recognised by the name of a shirt maker, that a victim had an eyeglass and, before the days of credit cards, Postal Order counterfoils provided identification. A passenger, Mr Newall, was identified by the surgical maker's name stamped inside an artificial body part.

The Harbour Board had experience of ships sinking in the Mersey, and initially it was expected that there would be groups of survivors, all wearing lifebelts, clinging desperately together in their struggle against the sea. However, when the early searches of the sea and the ship found no bodies, the idea gained ground that the crew had locked the passengers in their cabins as a safety precaution to prevent the sea washing inside. Indeed *The Times* of 6th December reported that as no bodies had been recovered it was supposed that 'the passengers were imprisoned in their berths'. On the other hand the absence of bodies supported

THE TIMES, MONDAY, DECEMBER 6, 1909.

THE WRECK OF THE ELLAN VANNIN.

THIRTY-THREE LIVES LOST.

It is now certain that the Ellan Vannin mail steamer, of the Isle of Man Steam Packet Company, which left Ramsey early on Friday morning for Liverpool, was wrecked, during the gale, at the mouth of the Mersey and that all on board have perished. There were in the vessel a crew of 21 and 12 passengers. The wreck of the steamer has been discovered in deep water at the bar entrance to the Mersey. Three Liverpool Dock Board tenders went to this point yesterday. At low water the mast of the vessel came into view about one mile from the Bar lightship and about 14 miles from the Liverpool landing stage. A diver was sent down to make an examination of the steamer, and upon his report the opinion was expressed that the Ellan Vannin had been swamped by a heavy sea and had apparently foundered in a few seconds.

There was no sign of any human bodies, although a careful search was made. It is stated that the vessel will not be blown up, but that an effort will be made to raise her.

A Ramsey telegram states that the Fenella arrived at Ramsey yesterday with the mails which the Ellan Vannin should have brought. The steamer had passed near the scene of the wreck, and those on board saw wreckage floating about in the sea. The opinion was expressed that the Ellan Vannin, being overwhelmed by heavy seas, heeled over and sank immediately. Her passage to the Bar was considered remarkable. As no bodies have been recovered, it is supposed that the passengers were imprisoned in their berths.

A portion of the captain's bridge has been washed ashore at New Brighton, and one of the steamer's lifeboats was found on the rocks close by. The boat was covered with canvas, and apparently had not been launched. Two more dead sheep were also washed up by the tide under the pier at New Brighton.

THE PASSENGERS.

The Steam Packet Company have issued the following complete list of the passengers who were on board the steamer :—

Mr. Higginbottom, Trafalgar Hotel, Ramsey.
Mr. and Mrs. Johnson, Beaconsfield Towers, Ramsey.
Mr. H. Joughlin, Thuro Cottage, Bridge, Isle of Man.
Mrs. Crix and child, of Ramsey.
Miss Fisher, Queen's Hotel, Ramsey.
D. Newell, 67, Hampton-road, Croydon, and W. Williams, 12, Walgrove-terrace, Earl's-court-road, London (stonemasons employed at the new Roman Catholic church at Ramsey).
A man unknown, said to be a farm labourer from the Isle of Man.
Two young women whose identity is not known.

THE TIMES OF 6TH DECEMBER WHICH GAVE AN EARLY ACCOUNT OF THE DISASTER. THE NUMBER OF PEOPLE LOST WAS INCORRECTLY REPORTED.

To the officers and crew who were called for duty in the greatest of all vessels on 3rd December 1909.

Anon.

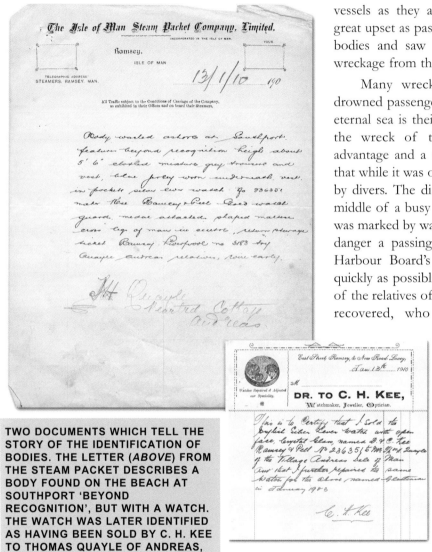

THE AFTERMATH OF THE DISASTER

The Isle of Man Steam Packet Company, Limited.

TWO DOCUMENTS WHICH TELL THE STORY OF THE IDENTIFICATION OF BODIES. THE LETTER (*ABOVE*) FROM THE STEAM PACKET DESCRIBES A BODY FOUND ON THE BEACH AT SOUTHPORT 'BEYOND RECOGNITION', BUT WITH A WATCH. THE WATCH WAS LATER IDENTIFIED AS HAVING BEEN SOLD BY C. H. KEE TO THOMAS QUAYLE OF ANDREAS, ONE OF THE PASSENGERS (*RIGHT*).

vessels as they approached Liverpool. There was great upset as passengers saw divers looking for the bodies and saw the occasional piece of floating wreckage from the *Ellan Vannin*.

Many wrecks remain on the seabed. The drowned passengers and crew remain there and the eternal sea is their grave. However, the location of the wreck of the *Ellan Vannin* was both an advantage and a disadvantage. The advantage was, that while it was on the seabed, it was easily reached by divers. The disadvantage was that it was in the middle of a busy shipping channel, and although it was marked by warning signals, there was always the danger a passing ship might collide with it. The Harbour Board's desire to remove the wreck as quickly as possible was in direct conflict with many of the relatives of those whose bodies had not been recovered, who wanted the wreck to be a consecrated grave. The dilemma of how to meet these competing wishes filled volumes of column inches in the newspapers. There were negotiations between the authorities and the Board, as well as much consideration by officials of the Steam Packet.

The Board's approach was that before blowing up the vessel, as a first step, the deck should be taken off. This would would have two advantages. It would make the sea clearer for other ships and it would be one further step to ensuring that there were no more bodies on the wreck. But on the Island rumours persisted. One said that the Harbour Board were going to blow up the wreck in secret to avoid the outrage of desecrating any remaining bodies. It was claimed that the most appropriate time to try and get away with this was when people's attention was directed towards other matters such as the pending General Election.

There were rumours to the opposite effect as well. The *Ellan Vannin* was never going to be blown up, it was claimed, because there was no need. She had

one theory as to the cause of the disaster. This theory was that the storm had smashed in the top of the saloon and the bodies had floated out into the sea.

Services between the Island and Liverpool had to continue. A fortnight after the disaster the Steam Packet chartered the 552 ton steel single-screw steamer *Elm*, considered to be the ideal short-term replacement for the *Ellan Vannin*. The *Elm* belonged to the Laird Line from Glasgow and was chartered for three months for the Ramsey to Liverpool run. There were many reports of distress, not only from passengers on the *Elm* but on other Steam Packet

FOUNDERING OF THE ELLAN VANNIN.

SUNK IN THE MERSEY ESTUARY.

APPALLING LOSS OF LIFE.

BODIES RECOVERED.

sunk in the sand and mud and was no longer a danger to shipping. But nothing feeds rumours more than a few false facts and in the New Year of 1910 a number of explosions were heard in the coastal communities surrounding Liverpool, which were put down to the secret blowing up of the wreck. Further support for the theory came when a number of bodies were found on the adjoining coasts later in January. It was claimed that the blowing up had released bodies trapped in the wreck, causing them to come to the surface and float to the shores. However, it later transpired that the explosions which had been heard were caused by something else altogether.

At one time the Harbour Board thought of raising the *Ellan Vannin*, but as she sank further and further into the sand and mud, this became less practicable. Early in 1910 the Steam Packet's Liverpool agents announced that there were no proposals to engage an independent diver to examine the wreck. The Company was quite content to rely on the conclusions reached by the Harbour Board's divers, that the *Ellan Vannin* had sunk following a collision.

Meanwhile, the Board was anxious to clear any wreckage that might have been an obstruction to shipping in the Channel as quickly as possible, and as soon as they were satisfied there were no more bodies to be recovered, they set about blowing up the two parts of the wreck. The work was completed on 6th April 1910.

Dealing with the the bodies or what remained of them was the responsibility of the relatives. Some bodies such as Miss Findlay's were returned home for interment. The Steam Packet directors agreed to meet not only the cost of Miss Findlay's father's travel expenses in coming to identify his daughter's body, but also the cost of conveying the body to London.

But not all claims were paid in full. For example, Mr Allen, whose wife and son were passengers, submitted an undertaker's bill of £19. The directors considered that the bill contained items that were excessive and which the Company could not reasonably be expected to pay. Instead of £19, only £10 was paid. Mr Allen's wife and son had travelled on a contract ticket which gave unlimited travel on the Company's vessels for a specified period of time. As both his wife and son were no longer able to use the ticket, Mr Allen approached the Steam Packet for a refund of the unused portion. After much debate, the claim was resolved with a fresh contract ticket being issued which would enable Mr Allen and two other members of the family to use it for a limited period.

FOUNDERING OF THE ELLAN VANNIN.

SUNK IN THE MERSEY ESTUARY.

APPALLING LOSS OF LIFE.

BODIES RECOVERED.

MANY ISLAND RESIDENTS WERE KEPT INFORMED OF THE UNFOLDING DRAMA BY NEWSPAPER REPORTS SUCH AS THE ONE ABOVE.

THE AFTERMATH OF THE DISASTER

NAME	DATE	CARGO	TONNAGE

ELLEN VANNIN — 3rd December 1909 — GROSS 380 — NET

LENGTH	BREADTH	DEPTH	POSITION, BAY OR RIVER	LATITUDE 53° 32′ 02″ N	S.S. (COAL OR OIL)	WOOD IRON OR STEEL
198	22	10	Square E.4	LONGITUDE 03° 16′ 54″ W	M.V. SAIL OR BARGE	

NATURE OF CASUALTY

Sank during the early morning of 3rd. about 1170 yds. about E by S¾S (Magnetic)
off the Bar Lightship. 35 lives lost.
Destroyed by M.D.H.B. Work completed 6th. April 1910
Charges: 3 - 100lbs; 1 - 150lbs; 63 - 300lbs.

DEPTH :- 30 FT. BELOW L.B.D =
315 061.9 E
8.6m BELOW C.D 75   404 928.6 N

THE CARD RECORDING THE BLOWING UP OF THE ELLAN VANNIN BY THE MERSEY DOCKS AND HARBOUR BOARD.

Captain Teare's body was found on the shore at Birkdale, near Southport, on 16th January 1910. The body of John Craine, the first mate, was found the next day on the shore at Southport. The return of bodies to the Island followed a similar pattern. A Steam Packet ship conveyed them from Liverpool to Douglas. The passengers and crew were in solemn mood as the ship's flag was at half mast for the journey. Invariably, as a ship bringing back a recovered body entered Douglas harbour, the police had to control the large crowds that were waiting. Hearses took the coffins, covered with Union Jack flags, to the deceaseds' homes to await the funerals. In the case of Captain Teare, it had been arranged that his body would travel to Douglas on board the Steam Packet's ship, *Douglas*. His widow's uncle, Captain Cowley, was the master of the ship for that day.

The funeral of Captain Teare and John Craine was a poignant occasion. Their bodies were interred together in Douglas Borough Cemetery. There were unparalleled scenes of sympathy on the day of the funerals. The blinds of all the houses on the route were closed. Approximately five thousand people watched the funeral procession. There were seven Steam Packet captains and the Company's General Manager immediately behind the hearse. Captain Keig, the Commodore of the fleet, led the captains, and other Steam Packet crew followed behind. The Chairman of the Company and two other directors were in the procession. Members of Captain Teare's Masonic Lodge and members of his family were also present.

At the funeral, members of the Lodge dropped a sprig of Acacia on the Captain's grave. A sprig of Thyme was placed on John Craine's grave by the Oddfellows. It was stated that the graves were contiguous as the officers had desired. They were probably on the bridge together when the ship went down. Certainly their bodies were recovered from similar spots.

The sad scenes were repeated throughout the Island as the bodies of other crew members were returned. Richard Clague was buried at Kirk Braddan Cemetery. There was a dreadful snow storm at the time and it was said it was ironic that not only should he have lost his life in a storm but should be buried in similar conditions. The only body of a passenger that would seem to have been brought back to the Island was that of Mr Quayle. A large crowd watched as his coffin was unloaded in Ramsey harbour from where a hearse took it to Andreas.

A number of inquests were held into the deaths following the sinking of the *Ellan Vannin*. The procedure was that the Coroner, whose jurisdiction extended over a particular geographical area, had the responsibility for summoning the jury if a body was found in that area. Quite often, the same witnesses who gave evidence at the inquests also gave evidence at the subsequent Board of Trade enquiry. At some of the inquests, including the first, the Steam Packet and the Mersey Docks and Harbour Board were represented by lawyers, but at other inquests there would seem to have been no legal representation for the Company or the Board.

The first inquest was held two weeks after the disaster on 17th December 1909 at the Dale Street police buildings in Liverpool. The inquest was into the

THE AFTERMATH OF THE DISASTER

deaths of the ship's cook, Mr Burke, and one of the passengers, Ernest Allen. The Steam Packet's early opinion was forcibly expressed by the fleet's Commodore, Captain Keig. Captain Keig thought that

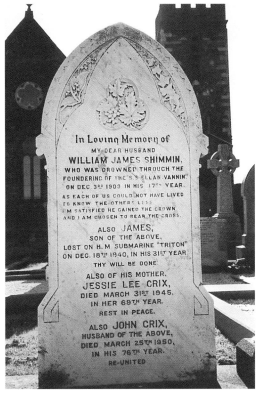

THE GRAVE OF WILLIAM SHIMMIN, A FIREMAN ON THE ELLAN VANNIN, IN ANDREAS CHURCHYARD. HE DIED BEFORE THE BIRTH OF HIS SON, JAMES, WHO ALSO DIED IN A TRAGEDY AT SEA.

no sea could have caused the damage sustained by the *Ellan Vannin*. He did not think she had been overwhelmed by the weather, she was too good a sea boat for that to happen. Further, the *Ellan Vannin*'s hull was double plated and she was built twice as strong as steamers were in 1909.

William Williams, the lookout on the Bar Lightship, gave evidence stating that two steamers had been seen at about 6.30am on 3rd December 1909. At the subsequent Board of Trade enquiry this time was revised to 6.00am and this was accepted. His principal evidence was that he had seen a third steamer which he thought was the *Ellan Vannin* on her way to Liverpool.

Lieutenant Mace from the Harbour Board gave evidence saying that he didn't think the *Ellan Vannin* had struck a mine. If the ship had, the damage would have been much greater. The inquest heard further evidence that the Q1 buoy had been found adrift with no sign of damage. The buoy was perfectly smooth, its light was burning and flashing correctly. There was no damage to the internal mechanism or indeed any sign of damage on the outside of the buoy. In view of this very positive evidence that the *Ellan Vannin* had not collided with the Q1 buoy, it is surprising that this possibility continually recurred throughout the subsequent Board of Trade enquiry.

The Coroner commenced his summing up to the jury by reminding them that if the men had drowned it was their job to find the cause of their drowning. After only five minutes' deliberation the jury returned their verdicts. The *Ellan Vannin* had been sunk following a collision. It should be added that the jury were not required to go into the details of what the *Ellan Vannin* had collided with or any further particulars of the collision. The Harbour Board were put on notice by the Coroner's direction that the proper authorities should be advised of the jury's conclusions.

The subsequent report to the full meeting of the Harbour Board concluded that the *Ellan Vannin* had been sunk following a collision. The background papers to support this conclusion would have made interesting reading but unfortunately it seems they were destroyed in the Second World War bombing of Liverpool.

There were vested interests in pursuing different theories for the sinking. The Harbour Board could be criticised if the *Ellan Vannin* had been sunk after colliding with submerged or hidden wreckage. Similarly, there was potential criticism of the Steam Packet if in fact the *Ellan Vannin* had been sunk after colliding with another vessel. Indeed, the Steam Packet would have been especially concerned to avoid any criticism. The 1894 Merchant Shipping Act restricted the Steam Packet's liability to certain specified maximum amounts. For a passenger's life the maximum was £15 per ton of the ship. For this purpose the tonnage of a ship was calculated

according to special rules. In respect of cargo, the limitation of liability was £8 per ton of the weight of the cargo. These limitations of liability however, did not apply if it could be shown that the Steam Packet had been at fault. Collision with another vessel might have suggested that there had been some error on the part of the captain which would have been the responsibility of the Steam Packet.

As more and more bodies were recovered from the coasts of Lancashire and Cheshire, arrangements were put in hand for the summoning of further inquest juries. Meanwhile, extensive correspondence was conducted between the Steam Packet, acting through their Ramsey agent, Mr Bell, and the Board of Trade, about the way the cargo was loaded. The *Ellan Vannin* was only carrying about a quarter of her permitted capacity but the Board of Trade were concerned that in some way the cargo may have been unevenly loaded or insecurely stowed in the holds. Either of these possibilities could have made the ship unsteady and might have accounted for her sinking. Further, of course, unsecured cargo moving in the hold could conceivably have damaged the sides of the ship and resulted in the ship being holed. It would seem as if the last copy of the original shipbuilder's plans was forwarded to the Steam Packet's Liverpool agents. Orford & Sons used these plans and Mr Bell's hand written plan of the position of the cargo to try and persuade the Board of Trade that the cargo had been correctly stowed.

The third body that was recovered from the wreck was that of John Taubman, a member of the crew. The inquest jury considered their verdict on 22nd December. The foreman of the jury delivered the verdict that 'Mr Taubman drowned through the sinking of the *Ellan Vannin*'. By implication the verdict meant that the jury felt there had been no collision. The *Ellan Vannin* had sunk because of the adverse weather. However, one juror disagreed and felt that the *Ellan Vannin* had sunk following a collision. After instruction from the Coroner and further deliberations, the jury returned and repeated their initial verdict with the following addition: 'there was evidently a collision, but there was no evidence to show with what it took place'. The Taubman jury's verdict was the first indication that the collision theory was losing credibility.

The verdicts into the deaths of Daniel Newall, a passenger, and Samuel Rydings, a crew member, followed shortly afterwards. The jury found that the two men had drowned through the *Ellan Vannin* sinking. There was no suggestion of a collision.

This verdict was quickly followed by the inquests into the deaths of Captain Teare and Miss Findlay, a passenger. This jury specifically disagreed with the collision theory and brought in a verdict that the deaths came about through the weather sinking the *Ellan Vannin*.

In subsequent inquests, the juries' verdicts were that the deceased lost their lives by drowning through the sinking of the *Ellan Vannin* and by implication the sinking came about because of the appalling weather.

By the time a jury were summoned to consider the deaths of Messrs Cannell and Stubbs, two crew members, the 'drowned through sinking' verdict was being referred to as the 'usual verdict'. Mr J C Bate, the West Cheshire Coroner, instructed the jury that 'If you are satisfied as to the identity of the two bodies (of which there could be no doubt) you should return the verdict that the deceased had drowned through the *Ellan Vannin* sinking. This

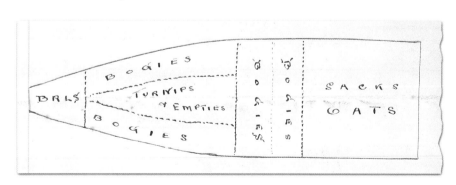

THIS PLAN OF THE DISTRIBUTION OF THE CARGO WAS PRESUMABLY DRAWN BY THE STEAM PACKET'S RAMSEY AGENT, JAMES BELL.

verdict has been reached by other inquest juries'. After a brief retirement the jury returned and delivered their verdict. As was to be expected, the jury, in effect, decided that the *Ellan Vannin* had sunk as a result of the weather.

One exception to the 'usual verdict' came when a Blackpool jury considered the cause of the death of John Cook, the member of the crew who came from Peel. This jury, perhaps because they were some distance away from the rumours circulating on Merseyside, felt they were unable to reach a conclusion as to what brought about Mr Cook's death. They returned an open verdict.

Many of the jurors throughout this harrowing period were released from further service on inquests.

Back on the Island, as the Manx nation received detailed accounts of these inquests through the local newspapers, there was endless discussion as to why the *Ellan Vannin* sank. Was it a collision or was the

ONE OF MANY LETTERS THAT WERE EXCHANGED IN THE AFTERMATH OF THE DISASTER ATTEMPTING TO SORT OUT THE PERSONAL BELONGINGS OF THE DECEASED.

weather responsible, or was there even some other explanation? As it became clear just how dreadful the storm was through which the *Ellan Vannin* had sailed, the possibility that the weather was responsible for her loss was spoken about by some seamen. One of the crew of the *Tynwald,* which had been called up for service to act as a stand-in after the loss of the *Ellan Vannin* said 'I knew every man on her. It would have been rough entering the river early on Friday morning. Rough! It would be a regular hell-kettle, that's what it would be'. He went on to explain that the seas would have been rolling like Snaefell behind the *Ellan Vannin* because of the 80 mile an hour wind to her stern. The ship would have met the five knot tide coming out of the Mersey. The seaman described what the effect would be. The sea would seethe and bubble, the bows of the *Ellan Vannin* would get tilted upwards and then the sea would flood the stern of the ship. He had seen this happen before. Water would be up to the sailors' shoulders and they would wonder whether the ship would ever come up again. One wave would follow another until the *Ellan Vannin* did not have a chance to rise, only the funnel and masts would be out of the water. His conclusion was that the *Ellan Vannin* had just been pushed under the sea and buried under the waves. The low stern of the *Ellan Vannin* would have been particularly susceptible to being weighed down by the sea. In the treacherous shallow waters of the approach to the Mersey, the *Ellan Vannin*'s propellers would have pulled her down aft making the swamping of the stern of the ship likely. His conclusion was clear: in the weather encountered by the *Ellan Vannin*, she would have been swamped like an open boat.

A popular theory at the time and one that is still held by some Steam Packet captains (though not all) is based on the fact that the *Ellan Vannin* was approaching Liverpool from Ramsey rather than Douglas. It is claimed that this approach would have taken her into shallower waters, though others said that this was irrelevant as both courses had converged at the point at which she sank.

Another possible cause of the *Ellan Vannin*'s demise was defective machinery. One of the Harbour Board's most experienced divers, Thomas White, had agreed to come out of retirement to make a special inspection of the *Ellan Vannin*. It was rumoured at the

time that the ship's machinery was to be the main focus of his attention. It was believed that he was going to see if either a boiler explosion or some other mechanical defect had caused the *Ellan Vannin* to sink. However, there is no report of him making any such find. Some had claimed that the *Ellan Vannin* had been damaged before she reached the Bar, possibly her rudder did not work. There were though, doubts about this theory. The doubters' view was that if the *Ellan Vannin* had been damaged before she got to the Bar she would have signalled to the lightship as she passed. There had been no such signal.

Newspapers reported at the time that the Steam Packet carried out an experiment to see if something was wrong with the *Ellan Vannin*'s steering gear. The details were not given in the press, but it seems that the experiment was carried out on the *Douglas* whilst she was close to the cattle jetty at Prince's landing stage. Quite how relevant the experiment on the *Douglas* was to what might have happened on the *Ellan Vannin* was never explained. However, after the experiment, attention turned to other possible causes of the *Ellan Vannin* sinking.

The geography of the position where the *Ellan Vannin* sank is important. The approach to Liverpool is a narrowing channel, with the Lancashire shore on the left and the Cheshire shore on the right. Treacherous sandbanks form either side of this channel through which a deep cut is kept giving a minimum depth, at that time, of 30 feet of water at low tide. This channel, the Queen's Channel, is the main access to Liverpool, but it does not take a straight line; rather, it takes a long, sweeping course, avoiding the Cheshire shore and hugging the Lancashire shore. The channel was shown by a double line of iron buoys, the first of which was the Q1 buoy. The buoys on one side of the channel were red and on the other side black. A ship approaching Liverpool therefore, would first make for the Bar Lightship (which was about a mile and a half to the seaward of the first two buoys marking the start of the channel) and then keeping between the buoys, make the long curved course into Liverpool.

Where the *Ellan Vannin* was found, sandbanks touched the channel on both sides and it was

suggested that a possible cause of the disaster was that the ship sank after touching a bank. Indeed, the January 1910 edition of the respected journal *The Marine Engineer and Naval Architect* gave support to this possibility. The journal considered that the damage found by the divers gave rise to the theory that the *Ellan Vannin* may have been lost by contact, not with another ship, but with a fixed object. That object, it suggested, was the base of the new revetment at the River Bar, upon which the Harbour Board's engineers were working. There was some support for this theory. She would have opened like a trap door and broken into two pieces. Further, many items of cargo that were stowed well below the surface were found floating in the river shortly after she sank.

But many, familiar with the treacherous conditions of a following wind meeting an outgoing tide, felt that there was no need to consider the theory of the *Ellan Vannin* sinking following collision with a bank or the revetment works. She was swamped by the waves until she was literally all under water. The passengers would have been below deck. When the vessel was submerged all the passengers and crew would have had no chance of survival.

The theory that the *Ellan Vannin* had collided with a buoy seems to have started after the Steam Packet's *Douglas* arrived in Liverpool later on the Friday that the *Ellan Vannin* sank. The captain of the *Douglas* reported that the Q1 buoy was missing. Those advancing this theory considered that if the *Ellan Vannin* was not answering her helm, owing to a breakdown in her steering gear or machinery, which was quite possible in the weather conditions, a collision with the Q1 buoy was possible, and this was something later considered by the Board of Trade enquiry. One possibility that seems never to have been considered though, was whether the chains of the buoy become entangled with the ship's propeller; did the entangled chain pull the *Ellan Vannin* down by her stern?

However, there was no disagreement with the view that the *Ellan Vannin* did not strike the Bar. It had been deepened recently to 48 feet to allow passage by all vessels at all tides.

As we have seen, the Steam Packet's first opinion was that the *Ellan Vannin* had sunk following

THE AFTERMATH OF THE DISASTER

a collision with another vessel. But a newspaper reporter asked the question 'did the other vessel go off like 'a road hog motorist?' The Company and its agents quickly put in hand enquiries to trace such a vessel. One of the few reports of these enquiries appeared in *The Times* on the Wednesday following the disaster, 8th December. It was simply reported that 'Steamers leaving Liverpool on Thursday night did not report any incident'. But any steamer that left on Thursday night would have been well out to sea before the *Ellan Vannin* was in the vicinity of the Bar the next morning. Whether *The Times* report is accurate or contained an error, somehow 'Thursday night' appearing in the report rather than 'Friday morning', is not known.

Although enquiries may have been made about some of the ships leaving Liverpool, the possibility of the *Ellan Vannin* being damaged before she reached the Mersey does not seem to have been considered. One of the many theories that was frequently referred to in Ramsey was that the *Ellan Vannin* had been in collision with a ship sometime after she left Ramsey but before she reached the Mersey. She had been kept afloat by virtue of her bulkhead until the wild seas at the Bar overwhelmed her. To prove or disprove this theory, enquiries would have to have been made of all ships in the Irish Sea at the time, but there is no record of such enquiries being made.

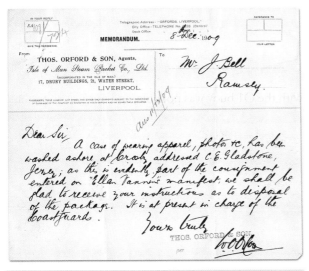

A LETTER SEEKING INSTRUCTIONS FOR THE RETURN OF AN ITEM FROM THE ELLAN VANNIN.

Another theory suggested that the *Ellan Vannin* had arrived safely at the Bar but was then in collision with a much larger ship. The larger ship was not damaged and in effect passed over the top of the *Ellan Vannin* cutting her in two. Apparently several liners left Liverpool at about the time of the disaster. In the appalling weather and with limited visibility, a large liner, many times the size of the little *Ellan Vannin*, may not even have appreciated that she had sunk the smaller ship.

A newspaper report at the time considered that it was in the interests of the Steam Packet to maintain that the *Ellan Vannin* had sunk as a result of a collision. Certainly this was the Steam Packet's view from the very beginning, and exactly how the *Ellan Vannin* sank intrigued a much wider audience than those immediately involved. The noted nautical magazine, *Shipping World* in its 8th December 1909 edition commented, 'how the crew and passengers of the *Ellan Vannin* met their fate will, forever, remain a mystery'.

Meanwhile, there were pressing matters for the Steam Packet to attend to. People were not as claims-minded in 1909 as they are today. However, in the words of the poem concerning Mrs Ramsbottom whose son had had his head bitten off at the zoo, 'someone was going to have to pay'. Many of the small items of cargo either belonging to passengers who were on the ship, or which had been sent unaccompanied, were recovered damaged. This extensive operation involved payments to the salvors, the Receiver of Wrecks, the coastguards and others responsible for recovery of the cargo. There were intricate arrangements for collection and distribution, usually by rail, to those entitled to the deceased's effects and other cargo. Mr Heaton Johnson's luggage, which was bound for India, had been sent well ahead and had arrived in France by the time the *Ellan Vannin* sank. Thomas Cook & Sons were responsible for retrieving the luggage from Marseilles and sending it back to Orford & Sons in Liverpool. Some of the damaged cargo was handed over to the Steam Packet's insurers, presumably for them to dispose of and get what money they could from its sale.

The majority of the claims would seem to have been referred to the directors of the Company for

them to decide what money should be paid, but there seems to have been little consistency in the way in which individual claims were handled. Some were turned down out of hand. The relevant entry in the directors' minute book merely stating that 'the application for compensation cannot be entertained'. Other requests for compensation were not dismissed but were held over for a later decision. What those later decisions were is not recorded.

The lost livestock had been shipped by farmers from Andreas, Bishopscourt and Bride. The oats, turnips and potatoes had been shipped by northern farmers as well as the Farmers' Combine Ltd. The farmers' live and dead stock was by far and away the most valuable cargo lost on the *Ellan Vannin* and much pressure was put on the Steam Packet for compensation. The Farmers' Combine, wholesalers in Liverpool, and the individual farmers all wrote in. The directors delayed a decision until 23rd December. The Company eventually decided that they were going to assume no liability. The losses had come about either because of an Act of God or another peril of the sea, and they were not responsible in these circumstances. The letter conveying this information caused an uproar. One of the farmers, Mr T B Cowley, acted as a representative on behalf of the shippers, and requested a meeting with the Steam Packet's directors. This was considered but the Board decided that as no compensation was payable under the terms of carriage, such a meeting was unnecessary. At the meeting of the Combine held on 18th March 1910 this response was discussed, and the directors resolved to 'use every endeavour to direct all its traffic from the Isle of Man Steam Packet Company for the future'.

Certainly the sinking did not seem to have deterred passengers from using the Steam Packet's services. Indeed, in February, Ramsey Town Commissioners had been complaining about the infrequent sailings to Ramsey and there were concerns about the Whitehaven service. The Commissioners requested a meeting with the Steam Packet's directors. A deputation from the Town Commissioners eventually attended a Board meeting on 3rd March. The Board reminded the Commissioners of the restrictions of a tidal harbour. The use of the Queen's Pier would have been of value for passenger-only vessels, and many Ramsey sailings were a mixture of cargo and passengers which would need to use the harbour. However, despite this, the directors promised that Ramsey services would be at least equal to those of previous years.

On 10th February 1910 the directors considered the launching arrangements for the Company's new ship, *Snaefell III*, and they also started to consider how to celebrate the anniversary of 80 years' service in August. One idea put forward was a parade of all the Company's ships, but before anything could be finalised the date for the Board of Trade enquiry into the sinking of the *Ellan Vannin* was announced. It was to start on 8th March. Would the enquiry's findings damage the Company's reputation? At the end of the enquiry would there be anything left to celebrate?

With these thoughts, the directors resolved who would look after the Company's interests at the enquiry, as they prepared for the most searching examination of its practices and procedures in the eight decades of its history.

CHAPTER EIGHT

THE ENQUIRY

Under the Merchant Shipping Act, 1894, the Board of Trade was empowered to set up a formal investigation into the loss of a ship. The investigations or enquiries were usually held in the port from which the lost vessel sailed or was closest for the convenience of the parties. Such enquires were presided over by a legally qualified chairman or, as he was called, President. The other members of the enquiry were usually ships' officers, often retired masters or captains, termed 'shipping assessors'. Board of Trade enquiry number 7338 into the sinking of the *Ellan Vannin* was held on 8th, 9th, 10th and 12th March 1910, at Dale Street Magistrates' Court, Liverpool. The President of the enquiry was Thomas Shepherd Little. Mr Shepherd Little was a barrister and a member of the Inner Temple. He seems to have had a largely undistinguished legal life for 35 years and he had been appointed a stipendiary magistrate for the City of Liverpool in 1908. He was assisted by three shipping assessors, the most senior of whom was Vice-Admiral Charles R Arbuthnot.

Vice-Admiral Arbuthnot had joined the Royal Navy as a cadet in 1863. He rose through the ranks to become a Rear-Admiral in 1904. The highlight of his career was the award of the Arctic Medal after his expedition to that continent as a lieutenant. He was also an Aide-de-Camp at King Edward VII's coronation in 1902. He retired from active service in 1907, but was promoted to Vice-Admiral the following year.

There were two other shipping assessors. Captain Henry Ellis Batt was born in Devon in 1850. He had had many years' foreign waters experience after gaining his first officer's certificate at Plymouth in 1871. In every year from 1900 to 1907 he had captained the *Ajax* to China, Japan and the oriental archipelago.

The other shipping assessor was Captain Owen Reynolds Mitchell who was born in Aberdeen in 1845. He was awarded his first officer's certificate in 1875. He too had experience in the Orient, having captained vessels to the East Indies, Burma and the Red Sea. He would seem to have last sailed in foreign waters in 1897.

Although he was a stipendiary magistrate and his prime duties would have been in the criminal courts, Mr Shepherd Little seems to have spent a lot of his time on shipping enquiries. He spent five days in January 1909 presiding over the enquiry into

SUMMONS TO THE STEAM PACKET'S RAMSEY AGENT, JAMES BELL, TO APPEAR AT THE BOARD OF TRADE ENQUIRY INTO THE SINKING OF THE ELLAN VANNIN.

'Sir', said the witness to the Chairman of the Enquiry,
'I don't know what to do'.
'Why, what is the matter?' asked the Chairman.
'I swore to tell the truth, but every time I try some
lawyer objects'.

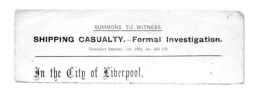

THE ENQUIRY

damage to the steam ship *Congress* and the loss of some of the crew, including the Captain. It would seem that the vessel had been prematurely abandoned by the Second Mate, who could have rendered assistance to three men washed overboard including the Captain and First Mate. The next month, February, four days were spent presiding over another enquiry about the damage, by stranding, to the *Belle of Ireland*. The following month, March, five days were spent investigating the loss of the sailing ship *Deccan* in Chile. Mr Shepherd Little's enquiries were all in Liverpool. Captain Batt, on the other hand, was very much a roving shipping assessor. In the previous 12 months he had assisted at enquiries in Cardiff, London and Liverpool.

The Steam Packet's interests at the enquiry were looked after by Mr Hughes-Games, a director of the Company. The Steam Packet's solicitors, Messers Bateson, Warr and Whimshurst of Liverpool, instructed a barrister to represent the Company. In an enquiry such as this it could reasonably be said that the Steam Packet's reputation was 'on the line'. The services of a good counsel were essential. The barrister briefed was Alexander Dingwall Bateson of the Inner Temple. He was a very experienced counsel who specialised in admiralty matters having practised from 2, King's Bench Walk in London for nearly 20 years. Mr Bateson was a junior, as opposed to a King's Counsel.

Both the Board of Trade and the Mersey Docks and Harbour Board were represented at the enquiry by local solicitors. Mr J Paxton, a partner in the firm Avison, Morton, Paxton & Co. and who had been a solicitor for nearly 40 years represented the Board of Trade; and William Calthrop Thorne represented the Mersey Docks and Harbour Board. He had over 20 years' experience and seems to have been employed full time by the Board.

The early part of the first day of the hearing on Tuesday 8th March was spent by Mr Bateson outlining the Steam Packet's case. Mr Bateson summarised the history of the *Ellan Vannin*'s last voyage so far as it was known, and the weather encountered by the ship as she approached the Mersey Bar. The Steam Packet's firm opinion, explained Mr Bateson, was that the

Ellan Vannin had struck some submerged wreckage. Skillfully, Mr Bateson tried to avoid any criticism of the Harbour Board. He suggested to the enquiry that it was possible that the ship struck submerged wreckage before reaching the Bar, outside of the area for which the Board were responsible.

An advocate wants to start a case with a good witness and there was no more imposing figure than the Steam Packet's General Manager, Mr William Corkhill. Mr Corkhill gave a detailed account of the *Ellan Vannin*'s history. He advised that, in the previous five years alone, over £5,300 had been spent on general upkeep, overhaul and repairs to the ship. At the time of the loss she was insured for £5,000. The Steam Packet were responsible for one seventh of the insured value leaving the insurers' liability as £4,286.

Mr Corkill stated that the Captain of the *Ellan Vannin*, Captain Teare, had been employed by the Company for 18 years. He had first been appointed to captain the *Ellan Vannin* in 1904 and thereafter there had been three promotions to larger ships before his final voyage on the *Ellan Vannin*. All of the ship's officers held masters' certificates. In other words, they were qualified to be the captain of the ship. Three of the crew, acting as ordinary seamen, held mates' certificates.

The Company had conducted every possible enquiry as to which vessel might have collided with the *Ellan Vannin*, but could not find such a vessel. Mr Corkhill suggested to the enquiry that the *Ellan Vannin* had not been in collision with another vessel but with something else.

Mr Bateson's second witness was Charles Blackburn, the Superintendent Engineer of the Steam Packet. Mr Blackburn was the Steam Packet employee most closely involved with the condition of the Company's ships. Much of his evidence was concerned with the condition of the *Ellan Vannin*'s plates. However, he was not able to tell the enquiry how many of the plates were originals and how many had been replaced. He did not expect the ship's plates to waste if they were well maintained. By 'well maintained' he meant kept clean, and he confirmed that the *Ellan Vannin*'s plates on both sides of the ship were regularly cleaned and painted.

THE ENQUIRY

The *Ellan Vannin* had been found to have broken in two and the line of the fracture was about 30 feet from the stern of the ship. Mr Blackburn did not think that it was possible for there to be a weakness in the plates where the fracture had occurred. He regularly inspected the *Ellan Vannin*, the last time being on 24th November. It was Mr Blackburn's responsibility to receive reports from captains and engineers of anything wrong with the Company's ships, but he had received no such report in respect of the *Ellan Vannin*. Because the ship had been fractured in its strongest part, it suggested that she had come into contact with a heavy object. That the divers also found the plates turned inwards suggested that the *Ellan Vannin* had been sunk after a collision. However, he did not think that the *Ellan Vannin* had collided with another ship. He pointed out that the damage was not extensive enough, and the plates were not turned in sufficiently for a collision with a ship to be the reason for the sinking. Furthermore, the *Ellan Vannin* had not suffered damage to the upper part of her structure which would have happened if the collision had been with another vessel.

Mr Blackburn's conclusion was, therefore, that the *Ellan Vannin* had collided with something that was submerged. He felt that the *Ellan Vannin*, having struck the submerged object, had been holed but did not sink at once. It was only after sinking that she broke into two pieces. He discounted that there had been a breakdown in the engine room or boilers because there had been no reported trouble, and he himself had found everything working and in good order when he carried out his last examination on 24th November, 10 days or so before the ship sank.

Mr Blackburn did not think he could be more positive as to what had happened to the *Ellan Vannin*. The bottom of the ship would tell the complete story. This was submerged in the sand of the Mersey and so he was unable to offer any further explanation.

Much of the remainder of Mr Blackburn's evidence concerned the thickness of the *Ellan Vannin*'s plates. Having confirmed that both the vessel and her plates were kept in the highest state of efficiency, he advised that the plates were in many cases 7/16 of an inch thick. However, some of the plates were 4/16 and 5/16 of an inch thick. The plates were predominantly two feet wide. As an illustration of the efficiency of the plates of the *Ellan Vannin*, Mr Blackburn advised that the ship had never suffered any leakage.

It was decided to adjourn for lunch before Mr Blackburn finished his evidence. The Steam Packet could be cautiously optimistic. From the Company's point of view they had had a reasonably satisfactory morning.

The enquiry resumed at 2.30pm and Mr Blackburn continued his evidence about the *Ellan Vannin*'s plates. Two plates had been replaced as a result of an accident in 1902 when the *Ellan Vannin* collided with a pier. There had also been some new plates fitted since then to replace ones that were wearing out. All of the new plates fitted were 7/16 of an inch thick. The *Ellan Vannin*'s bottom was often inspected when the ship was in Douglas at low tide and was resting on the harbour bed. Mr Blackburn concluded his evidence by stating that he had never known the *Ellan Vannin* to turn back from the Bar due to bad weather.

The next witness, Lieutenant Hugh Williams, the senior assistant water bailiff to the Mersey Docks and Harbour Board, dealt with some of the pre-enquiry speculation that the *Ellan Vannin* had been sunk because she had collided either with the Q1 buoy or with the iron chains which secured the buoy to the sea bed. His firmly expressed evidence was that the *Ellan Vannin* could not have collided with the buoy. Certainly the buoy had broken away from its proper location, but due to the state of the tides and where the buoy was found, it was not possible for the *Ellan Vannin* to have collided with it and broken it free from its moorings.

The enquiry then heard the evidence of the Marine Superintendent and Commodore of the Steam Packet's fleet, Captain Keig. Captain Keig was a much respected figure. He had captained every ship in the Company's fleet. He was a thorough master of nautical construction and indeed, a Lloyd's surveyor once commented that no one knew more about the practical details of ships than Captain Keig. The

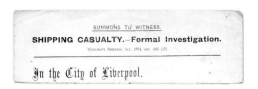

THE ENQUIRY

Captain advised that the ship's plates were kept in good condition and repair, and were painted inside and outside twice a year. There had been a good deal of new plating fitted when the *Ellan Vannin* was converted from a paddle steamer in 1883 and also during the special overhaul at the Naval Armament and Construction works in Barrow in 1891. Captain Keig could not say if the fracture occurred in the original plating or in plating that had been fitted later.

He was firmly of the opinion that the *Ellan Vannin* struck submerged wreckage or something else under the water causing damage to the bottom of the ship on the port side. He came to this conclusion because the *Ellan Vannin*'s keel was bent upwards and also from the divers' description of her indented plates. He believed the ship fractured after having the collision which holed her, and as she filled with water she broke in two.

Captain Keig was able to confirm that on Tuesday 30th November, three days or so before the disaster, the ship's steering gear was in good order. There had been no trouble with the *Ellan Vannin*'s steering gear for years.

Captain Keig had been captain of the *Ellan Vannin* before her conversion and he asserted that she was the best little ship that he had ever been on. With only carrying a quarter of her permitted cargo, she would have been in splendid trim and should have withstood any sort of weather.

Despite this ringing endorsement, Captain Keig was not able to leave the witness box without having to answer further questions about the *Ellan Vannin*'s plates. He felt that the plates were stronger than those being put in modern vessels and he did not think that they had corroded. He was able to confirm various details. The water ballast tank was not used but it was watertight. The steering gear was in the Captain's house, and as far as repairs to the *Ellan Vannin*'s rudder were concerned, these had taken place in 1895 and 1897. The repairs were due to ordinary wear and tear.

After Captain Keig had finished his evidence Thomas Millar was called. He was the Board of Trade's engineer and surveyor at Liverpool. Mr Millar had surveyed the *Ellan Vannin* five times in all, the first time in 1905, and the last in September 1909.

So far as the September survey was concerned, he had conducted an external examination on 11th September when the ship was in dry dock in Liverpool. The internal examination of the ship had taken place in Douglas on 14th and 15th of September. The *Ellan Vannin*'s plates had been examined as part of the dry dock examination. He found the surface plates to be in good condition. In the chain locker, he had examined the plates on both sides and also found these to be in good condition. There was some wasting of the plates but this was not material, and some portions of the plates were as good as new. Overall, the condition of the plates was good and there was no sign of weakness.

In respect of the *Ellan Vannin*'s machinery, he found this to be in good order also. Mr Millar then gave evidence about the life saving equipment that was available. There were two lifeboats which could hold 38 people, 320 lifebelts and six lifebuoys, in addition to floating seats which held 18 people. By way of alerting other ships or lookouts of any distress, the *Ellan Vannin* carried rockets, 12 blue lights and two deck flares. There was an adequate supply of signals on board. Mr Millar then turned to the light that had been seen from the Bar Lightship. He felt that the white and greenish flare, which was reported to come from the *Ellan Vannin*, could have been from one of the ship's 12 blue lights. After his last survey he had commented to Captain Keig that the *Ellan Vannin* was 'a ship with a good many years life left in her.'

The President of the enquiry, Mr Shepherd Little, asked some questions concerning the adequacy of the life saving equipment. The President started with the position that although the Board of Trade had permitted the *Ellan Vannin* to carry 313 persons there were only lifeboats for 38 persons and floating seats for 18.

Mr Millar's response to the inadequacy of the life saving equipment was that it was sufficient according to the regulations issued by the Board of Trade. What went unsaid, was that the majority of the passengers and crew who could not get into the lifeboats or floating seats would have had to float in the Irish Sea until they were picked up. Assuming, that is, that they did not die of exposure in the meantime. There were, after all, sufficient lifebelts and lifebuoys

THE ENQUIRY

for all passengers. It was not until after the enquiry into the loss of the *Titanic* in 1912, that the regulations changed. Thereafter, a ship had to carry sufficient lifeboats for every passenger and member of the crew to be accommodated.

Mr Millar confirmed that none of the cement on the *Ellan Vannin* was broken. If it had been, that might have affected the trim of the ship. The cement was unbroken despite the fact that she was grounded on the bed of the harbour every day. He closed his evidence by confirming that the *Ellan Vannin* was a strong ship.

After Mr Millar, the next witness was Master Alfred Billet, a former captain of the *Ellan Vannin*. He had made between 600 and 800 winter passages across the Irish Sea in the *Ellan Vannin,* and had never had trouble whilst on her; she had never let in any water. Master Billet considered that there was not a finer little boat sailing out of the Mersey in all weathers. The *Ellan Vannin* behaved particularly well in bad weather. His evidence closed with a formal identification of the *Ellan Vannin*'s clock. A clock had been recovered from the shore at Blundellsands near Crosby, about six miles to the north of Liverpool. The hands had stopped at 6.50am. Master Billet recognised the clock as that of the *Ellan Vannin*. The clock was normally on a panel facing anyone entering the Captain's room.

The enquiry then heard from Master William Cain who was captain of the *Ellan Vannin* for his month's winter service in November 1909. When his service ended he handed over to Captain Teare, the day before the disaster. He described the *Ellan Vannin* as a 'nice little sea boat that behaved well in bad weather'. His brief evidence ended with him describing the location of the lifebelts. There were 18 in the companionway and 49 in the saloon. There were others in steerage and the rest were divided between the officers and crew.

The next witness was Stephen Looney. Mr Looney stove (helped load) the *Ellan Vannin* before she left Ramsey on 3rd December 1909. He was responsible for the stowage of 60 tons of cargo. He confirmed that the cargo was packed so that it would not shift or bang against the sides of the vessel no

matter how rough the weather. He was able to confirm that the *Ellan Vannin*'s draught was 10 feet aft and 7 feet 6 inches forward. When fully loaded the ship's draught was 10 feet 9 inches aft and 8 feet 9 inches forward.

James Bell, the Steam Packet's Ramsey agent, followed. He was on the quay when the *Ellan Vannin* left Ramsey and shortly before had remarked that the glass (barometer) was very low. To this comment Captain Teare had replied that he felt the reading on the glass indicated that snow was likely. However, he made no suggestion that the weather was too bad to go. Captain Teare was a cautious man. The decision on whether to sail was, of course, the Captain's, but Mr Bell also thought that the weather was not sufficiently adverse for the ship to be delayed. Mr Bell closed his evidence by informing the enquiry that he had sailed on the *Ellan Vannin* as cargo superintendent during his career. He felt she was a very good sea boat. Mr Bell was the last of the Steam Packet's employees called to give evidence.

The next witness was Master James Kewley, who was in charge of the Bar Lightship, which at the time was named *Planet*. About 6.00am he had seen two inward bound steamers. The first he presumed was from Belfast and the second from Dublin. The wind and mist prevented him from seeing Q1 buoy.

Later, one of his seaman, Williams, brought him on deck. Williams, who was on duty as lookout, thought that he had seen a distress flare from a ship. Master Kewley always liked to wait for the second distress signal. He preferred to make sure that what had been seen was, in fact, a distress signal. There was no instruction in his rule book that he should wait for two distress signals, it was just his preferred practice. If he had seen a second distress signal he would have set off the signals to alert the lookout on the coast to launch a lifeboat. At the time the sea was as bad as he had seen in 20 years' service. The lifeboat on the Bar Lightship could not have been launched in a sea of that ferocity.

The last distress signal he had observed was approximately two years ago when he had seen one long flare. On that occasion, he immediately launched the signals for assistance. He was asked why he did not

SUMMONS TO WITNESS.
SHIPPING CASUALTY.—Formal Investigation.
Merchant Shipping Act. 1894, sec. 466 (10).

In the City of Liverpool.

THE ENQUIRY

launch the signals immediately this time. He replied that he wanted to be sure that his seaman, Williams, was not mistaken. It was not that he did not trust Williams, he just wanted to be sure. He did not think that what Williams had seen had been a signal from a ship for a pilot boat, but was a signal from a vessel in distress. The question remained unanswered, if he thought there was a ship in distress, why wait?

Master Kewley was the last witness at the end of the first day's proceedings and the Steam Packet could look back on a first day that, from their point of view, had gone extremely well. No doubt as he made his way back to his hotel, Mr Bateson hoped that the second and subsequent days would be just as successful.

The second day of the enquiry started promptly on the morning of Wednesday 9th March at 10.30. William Williams, the seaman on the Bar Lightship, was called to give evidence. Mr Williams confirmed that at the relevant time he was the lookout on the lightship. The sea was very high and there was a force 11 wind from the north-west. Mr Williams told the enquiry that although he could see the Formby Lightship he could not see the red flashing light of the Q1 buoy. He could see many red lights but these might have been from other buoys and he was not able to say if the Q1 buoy was adrift.

At about 6.30am Mr Williams saw the masthead light of an inward bound steamer coming from the north. It was about half a mile away from the Bar Lightship and he had it in view for five minutes or so. There was then a heavy shower which obscured the light. He next saw a flash lasting for about half a second in the vicinity of the Bar in an east south-easterly direction from the Bar Lightship. He assumed, from the direction of the inward steamer and the position of the flash, that this had come from the steamer.

He called his skipper, Master Kewley, who said that they should wait for a second flash from the steamer. Both he and Master Kewley laid out the signals on the deck so that they were ready to launch. They waited for 20 minutes but neither of them saw

any second flash. The lawyers tried to find out if what he had seen was a distress signal or flare. Mr Williams described how he would distinguish a 'flare' from a 'flash'. A flare would last for quite a long time whereas a flash would only last for a second.

He was cross-examined about the evidence he had given at the inquest which had been held on 17th December, presumably the inquest into the deaths of the passenger Ernest Allen and Edward Burke, the *Ellan Vannin*'s cook. At that inquest he described what he had seen as a 'flare'. In fact, in the lightship's logbook the description of what he had seen was recorded as a 'flare-up'. Despite lengthy cross-examination, clarification of exactly what Mr Williams saw was not resolved. Cross-examination then continued as to the time the sighting had occurred. He maintained that he saw the flash at approximately 6.45am. Again, he was closely questioned about conflicting evidence he had given at the inquest when he was said to have claimed that he had seen the flash at 7.15am. He maintained that this was incorrect and that what he had seen had happened at 6.45am.

A captain of one of the inward bound steamers that had been observed from the Bar Lightship then gave evidence. Master Arthur Porter was captain of the *Heroic*. He passed the Bar Lightship at about 6.00am. The sea raged as if there was a hurricane. It was very high, broken and dangerous, especially between the Bar Lightship and the Q2 buoy (this was further inwards towards Liverpool than the Q1 buoy). In 11 years of doing the Belfast to Liverpool crossing he had never seen the sea as bad as it was on this morning. The Q1 buoy was in position and having identified it he decided to go into Liverpool. The sea gradually got worse until he passed the Formby Lightship which was further inland than the Q1 and Q2 buoys. After passing the lightship the sea got better. He confirmed that the worst of the sea was between the Bar Lightship and the Q2 buoy. He met no ships either inward or outward on the way into Liverpool. He explained the importance of the Q1 buoy as marking the start of the dredged cut to Liverpool.

Returning to the conditions, he described how his ship was inclined to broach to at the Bar and take

SUMMONS TO WITNESS.
SHIPPING CASUALTY.—Formal Investigation.
MERCHANT SHIPPING ACT, 1894, SEC. 466 (10).

In the City of Liverpool.

THE ENQUIRY

up the whole width of the channel. This would have meant the ship was side on to the direction of the wind and the tide. In normal circumstances his ship was a good steering ship. With the wind and sea behind him they pooped heavy water three times. 'Pooping water' is a description of the sea when a ship is not matching its progress with that of the waves to the extent that the stern of the ship is covered with water.

After Master Porter, Sydney Harrison gave evidence. He was one of the coastguards at Blundellsands. Mr Harrison described how, in the early hours of the morning of 4th December, he found on the shore dead sheep and a number of lifebelts marked '*Ellan Vannin*'. He also found a piece of panelling on which was a clock. The clock did not appear to have been run down but had stopped at 6.50am.

The enquiry then heard evidence from Margaret Wilson who lived at the old lighthouse at Hightown towards Southport. Margaret Wilson's evidence about what she found is one of the most intriguing aspects of the *Ellan Vannin*'s sinking. Margaret Wilson described how, on 17th January 1910, she found a corked bottle on the shore near where she lived. She broke the bottle as she could not uncork it. Inside was a message written on a ruled sheet of paper which would seem to have come from a notebook. The message read 'Ellan Vannin been in collision with unknown steamer. Just going down. Good-bye to all. E Burke.'

The bottle did not seem to have been washed up that day because the water had not come up that far. She took the bottle and the message to the police. Mr E Burke, it will be recalled was the *Ellan Vannin*'s cook. The next witness to give evidence was Edgar Burke, the cook's son, who was a painter by occupation. He was familiar with his father's handwriting. He'd looked at the message from the bottle and thought that it had been written by his father. He didn't think the message was in his father's ordinary handwriting due to the circumstances in which the message was written, but he thought the signature did seem to be 'more like my father's ordinary handwriting'. He produced two postcards to the enquiry, one of which was to him and the other

was to Mrs Burke, to corroborate his evidence about who had written the message. He was satisfied the message was from his father.

Then Mr Burke gave what was probably the most significant piece of evidence that the enquiry heard. He confirmed that his father had a note book with ruled pages similar to the page on which the message in the bottle had been written. His father was in the habit of using pages from the notebook to send notes to him.

Mr Burke was questioned about whether his father had a bottle in his possession. To some extent to ask if the late Mr Burke possessed a bottle was a somewhat superfluous question. He was the ship's cook, and one is reasonably safe in assuming he would have access to many bottles.

However, after much verbal jousting with the lawyers, Mr Burke was able to confirm that his father had often said to him that in a storm, he would leave his last message in a bottle which he would throw overboard. For some reason the President, Mr Shepherd Little, decided to try and quash the idea that this message had actually been written by Mr Burke. He made the surprising and uninvited observation that no doubt some person had seen Mr Burke's signature and had written this message out on a piece of paper. The message itself did not seem to be in the same writing as that of the signature, although it was not a bad imitation. The President continued 'the person who had written this message seems to have said to himself 'I cannot imitate what I've never seen, but I'll try. I can however imitate the signature that I have seen' and that would account for the signature being, in the words of Edgar Burke, 'more like his father's writing''.

It is a principle of all judicial hearings, particularly one looking into the deaths of 35 people, that the Judge, or President of the enquiry hearing the evidence, makes a decision on that evidence alone and that members of the enquiry do not give evidence themselves. The President seems to have forgotten this basic rule of how judicial proceedings should properly be conducted. He gave evidence himself and contradicted the direct evidence of Mr Burke who was satisfied that the message had been written by his father.

SUMMONS TO WITNESS.
SHIPPING CASUALTY.—Formal Investigation.
Merchant Shipping Act, 1894, sec. 466 (10).

In the City of Liverpool.

THE ENQUIRY

None of the advocates either had the courage or felt inclined to disagree with the President of the enquiry. Indeed Mr Paxton, on behalf of the Board of Trade, regarded the issue as finished having heard the President's views. No one pursued the more obvious questions, such as how common were notebooks with ruled pages like that owned by Mr Burke's father? and no one suggested forwarding the message to an accepted handwriting expert. For absolute certainty, Mr Paxton lamely asked that if the enquiry were satisfied that the message was a hoax, he presumed that they did not wish to pursue the subject further. The President agreed. The paper label on the bottle (which was an HP Sauce bottle) showed no signs of having been in the water for a long period, and therefore the President confirmed that the message was a cruel hoax of a kind that, sadly, often happened after shipping accidents.

The enquiry then moved on to hear from the witnesses who found the *Ellan Vannin* after she had sunk. The first witness was John Lewis, the Master of the number two pilot ship. For those unfamiliar with pilot boats, these are the boats that were on duty in the approaches to the docks at Liverpool. A pilot guides ships unfamiliar with the approaches to their destination, and would similarly escort any outgoing ship to the open sea. Master Lewis confirmed that on 3rd December the weather was at its worst at about 4.00am. The weather was so bad that if any ship had been in distress he could not have assisted. At 6.00am the wind was at force 11 and blowing from the north-west.

He located the wreck of the *Ellan Vannin* at about midday on Saturday 4th December. He had seen a mast protruding out of the water. He did not know of any derelict and submerged vessel with which the *Ellan Vannin* could have collided. The barometer had been falling since Thursday 2nd December and the morning that the *Ellan Vannin* sank it was as low as it could go.

Next William Hicks, a New Brighton coastguard, told the enquiry about what he found by the rocks on which the lighthouse stood. Mr Hicks discovered what seemed to be *Ellan Vannin*'s starboard lifeboat at 6.30am on Saturday 4th December. When the lifeboat had come ashore its cover was on, all

tanks were in it and all the gear was out of the boat (although this evidence seems inconsistent with what had been reported ealier, particularly regarding what was inside the lifeboat).

After Mr Hicks the enquiry heard from the divers who had explored the *Ellan Vannin*. First to be called was Thomas Oliver White, who was a diver with the Mersey Docks and Harbour Board. He first went down to the *Ellan Vannin* on Sunday 5th December. He confirmed Mr Hicks' findings to the extent that there was more indication that the starboard lifeboat, as opposed to the port lifeboat, had been launched. Conditions were bad and he made no further discoveries. When he resumed the following day he found that the ship was fractured and in two pieces. He traced the fracture across the deck from one side to the other, and it was pretty straight. On the port side of the hull some of the plates had been bent inwards. He continued diving on the instructions of the Board and on 9th December found a seaman's body under a table in a cabin (although this evidence contradicts earlier reports that the body been found in the saloon). He later found the body of a boy in a cabin. These bodies were later identified to be those of the ship's cook, Mr Burke and Ernest Allen, a passenger. On another dive, on 13th December, he found a body in the engine room. This must have been the body of one of the ship's firemen, John Taubman.

Mr White was cross-examined by Mr Bateson on behalf of the Steam Packet about the line of severance of both parts of the ship. Mr White stated that the line of the fracture was about 30 feet from the ship's stem. The line was fairly straight. However, in one place on the port side in both sections of the ship, the plates were bent inwards for two to three feet. If both parts of the ship had been put together they would show a hole on the port side about four to six feet in size in the sheer strake and the strake below it (the strakes are the continuous lines of planking or plates from the stem to stern of a ship).

Mr White's opinion was that the ship's condition could only have been brought about by the vessel striking something. He was subject to lengthy cross-examination about the details of his findings, especially his measurements. More precise figures

SUMMONS TO WITNESS.
SHIPPING CASUALTY.—Formal Investigation.
MERCHANT SHIPPING ACT, 1894, sec. 466 (10).

In the City of Liverpool.

THE ENQUIRY

were not really elicited because, as Mr White explained, to measure the distances he used only his hands. Perhaps surprisngly, Mr White was not asked to explain why his estimate of the size of the hole was much less than the fourteen feet reported in the Steam Packet statement issued on 6th December after the divers' first inspection of the wreck.

Mr White accepted that the *Ellan Vannin* could have been in collision with a vessel. He had examined many wrecks that had sunk following collisions in his 21 years diving. Not all members of the enquiry appreciated the difficulties the divers were working under: the poor visibility and the constant fear of an airline being snagged on the wreckage. Once again the President intervened and forcibly asked Mr White what was likely to have struck the *Ellan Vannin*. Mr White could not add anything to what he said earlier. The President commented sarcastically that, according to Mr White's evidence, what struck the *Ellan Vannin* could have come 'from the sky above or the waters below or indeed anywhere on earth'. Despite pressing Mr White further, his answer remained the same: that he would not like to say anything else. But he accepted that at one time he thought the *Ellan Vannin* may have been in collision with another ship. Now his opinion was less certain. Perhaps, in his anxiety caused by the President's sarcasm, he lacked the confidence to be more definite.

In any event, before the President could continue his questioning of Mr White, two of the shipping assessors, Vice-Admiral Arbuthnot and Master Batt, intervened. The shipping assessors wanted to return to uncontroversial matters about the foremast and rigging of the ship. There was no dispute with Mr White's observations that he did not think that the loose foremast that he had found, had struck the plates and caused them to be indented. Mr White could not have left the witness box more quickly.

He was followed by Richard Walker Lawson. Mr Lawson was from Messrs Gibney & Co., a firm of divers, and he described the results of his examination of the *Ellan Vannin*. He had examined many ships after they had collided. He agreed with Mr White that the *Ellan Vannin* had either struck something or been struck by something but he could not suggest what. He agreed that at an earlier inquest he had expressed

the opinion that the *Ellan Vannin* had been in collision with another vessel. However, on reflection, whilst he was still of the opinion that the *Ellan Vannin* had been in collision with something, he had become less certain that it had been another ship.

Mr Lawson came to the conclusion that there must have been a collision judging by the type of damage that the *Ellan Vannin* had suffered. The common-sense view must be that the ship would not have broken in two parts unless there had been a collision. The shipping assessor, Master Batt, suggested to Mr Lawson that if the *Ellan Vannin* was moving when she had been struck by another vessel the fracture would have shown a different shape. There would have been more horizontal than vertical damage. The horizontal damage would have come about because the break would not have happened immediately the *Ellan Vannin* was struck. Because she was moving at the point of collision the other vessel would have moved along the side of the *Ellan Vannin* causing horizontal damage. Mr Lawson was not impressed with this logic. He felt that in the event of another ship striking the *Ellan Vannin* the damage might be either horizontal or vertical. Much would depend upon the size of the other ship, its shape, and the angle at which it hit the *Ellan Vannin*, as well as the speeds of both vessels.

Once again the President did not want to be kept out of the action, but on this occasion his intervention made a valuable point. He wondered aloud to the enquiry whether the new plates fitted to the *Ellan Vannin* bent as the vessel went down. The new plates may have been more flexible than the old ones. The bends or indentations could have been caused by the twisting of the vessel as she sank. The experts were left to think over this possibility but it does not seem to have been referred to again.

The last witness of the second day was William Carter, a diver and the Master of the Mersey Docks and Harbour Board's ship, *Salvor*. Mr Carter had also examined the *Ellan Vannin* and felt that the plates had not bent inwards but in some way had buckled. Mr Carter saw nothing to indicate that the *Ellan Vannin* had been in a collision. If there had been a collision he would have expected the damage to have been greater. His theory as to the cause of the loss of the *Ellan*

THE ENQUIRY

Vannin was that the skylight or entrance to the saloon was washed away in a heavy sea. She then filled with water and went down stern first. That the *Ellan Vannin* went down stern first was shown by the fact that the aft part of the ship was stuck in 13-14 feet of mud.

After this the bow would be in the air, protruding above sea level. The force of the sea meeting air in a solid place, the bow of the ship, would cause the bow to come apart from the stern. He had seen similar results where other ships had gone down by the stern leaving the bow out of the sea in the air. The wind and sea hitting the bow caused it to break off. He was firmly of the opinion that if the *Ellan Vannin* had struck a submerged object the fracture would have been horizontal and not vertical.

The second day of the proceedings ended after Master Carter's evidence, but the first seeds of the enquiry's eventual conclusions had been laid by him. Another satisfactory day for Mr Bateson and the Steam Packet. However, as the barrister conferred with his clients, it was apparent to all that the collision theory had been discredited. Master Carter's articulate evidence was largely unchallenged. He had given the enquiry, what was described as 'a believable explanation' for the loss.

The third day of the proceedings, Thursday 10th March, commenced at the later time of 11.00am. The Bar Lightship's Master, James Kewley, was recalled. Master Kewley confirmed that the full entry in the log book was, 'observed a flare-up in vicinity of Bar for about a minute'. He was not accustomed to seeing flares which would have indicated vessels were in distress. The only flares he was used to seeing were blue flares indicating that a pilot was required.

Before Master Kewley was able to leave the witness box the subject of the Q1 buoy was raised again. He advised that in his 25 years' service about 30 buoys had come adrift. However, he had never known a buoy come adrift because of a vessel colliding with it. All the buoys that had come adrift were as a result of the stress of the weather when the rough seas had caused the anchoring chains to snap.

The proceedings continued with the recall of another witness who had given evidence much earlier, Captain Keig. He was recalled to confirm that he was present when the first body, that of the ship's cook, Mr Burke, was brought to the surface. To Captain Keig, it looked as if the cook had been woken from his sleep because he was not fully clothed. It was suggested that an alternative explanation for Mr Burke's body not being fully clothed was that he might have taken off his clothes to swim for safety. Mr Burke's body was found in a cabin and Captain Keig commented that it was an unusual place for Mr Burke to be at that time of the morning. He should have been in the galley getting breakfasts ready for the passengers.

One of the Mersey Docks and Harbour Board's most senior officials, the Marine Surveyor and Water Bailiff, Lieutenant F W Mace was called to give evidence. Lieutenant Mace was a much respected figure in Liverpool. Merely by themselves, his office and position commanded attention. Lieutenant Mace's evidence was that at the time the *Ellan Vannin* sank the sea was so dangerous that if there had been distress signals from the vessel no lifeboat could have gone to her assistance. The north-westerly wind meeting the outgoing tide had made the conditions extremely treacherous.

Lieutenant Mace explained what he thought had brought about the disaster. The *Ellan Vannin* was in shallow waters. It was a well known fact that when a ship was in shallow water the length of the sea decreased and the height of the waves correspondingly increased. In other words, there was not the depth of water to absorb the winds encountered by the *Ellan Vannin*. In addition, the outgoing tide meeting wind from the opposite direction raised the height of the waves.

Lieutenant Mace was critical of Captain Teare. The Lieutenant's view was that Captain Teare had failed to appreciate the state of weather at the Bar. It was an error of judgement in trying to cross the Bar under these conditions. The correct course for Captain Teare to have taken was to round up. In other words, not to proceed any further but to wait until daylight. In daylight Captain Teare would have been in a better position to have steered the *Ellan Vannin* into

THE ENQUIRY

deeper water. He would also have been better able to appreciate the location of the banks on either side of the channel. Further, by this time, the conditions would have improved. However, Lieutenant Mace did not suggest that Captain Teare had hit a bank causing the *Ellan Vannin* to sink. Perhaps Lieutenant Mace realised that his criticisms might not stand detailed examination, because he quickly added that although the *Ellan Vannin* had been running for 50 years she would not have encountered conditions like those of 3rd December before.

Lieutenant Mace referred to the captain of the *Heroic* saying that his ship had sheered about badly. Because the *Ellan Vannin* was a much smaller vessel than the *Heroic* it was likely that she too had sheered about, making it difficult for Captain Teare to keep control. In Lieutenant Mace's opinion the *Ellan Vannin* broached to either because she yawed to windward or she took a very heavy sea which disorganised her steering gear. If a ship is lying on an advancing wave, i.e. surfing, she is likely to be slewed violently, keeled over and swamped. This process is termed 'broaching to'. Lieutenant Mace was of the opinion that the ship took a heavy sea on her stern, the after companion was swept away and she filled aft and sank. The stern of the vessel being embedded in 13 feet of mud supported his theory. The deck structure and size of the after hatchway made the *Ellan Vannin* especially susceptible to a large inflow of water in the event of the stern being damaged by heavy seas. Further, he claimed, it was often a feature of sinkings in the River Mersey that ships went down stern first with their bows remaining out of the water. Such ships were often in that position for a long time. He quoted an example from elsewhere: the submarine *C11*, which had sunk off the Norfolk coast in July 1909, had remained in this position for some weeks. (It is interesting to note that Lieutenant Mace was in fact wrong about this, the records of the Submarine Museum in Portsmouth, show that the *C11* sank in less than 40 seconds. Nothing of the vessel remained above sea level).

This stern first sinking is what had happened to the *Ellan Vannin*, felt Lieutenant Mace. The bow of the ship was buffeted by very heavy seas and she then broke in two, albeit in the strongest part of the ship.

The stern would remain in the mud and the bow would then sink a short distance away as had happened.

Lieutenant Mace also considered other reasons for the sinking. Sea striking under the *Ellan Vannin*'s forecastle head might have caused some weakness and perhaps a slight fracture. Such a fracture could have come about either on this voyage or a previous one. However there was no suggestion that the *Ellan Vannin* was inherently weak. The fact that the *Ellan Vannin* was nearly 50 years old was irrelevant; the quality of iron was better when the *Ellan Vannin* was built than it was in 1909. To encourage the enquiry not to spend too long on other theories Lieutenant Mace gave the Steam Packet a ringing endorsement. The Company's boats were considered to be the best maintained in the world and no ships of any company were better fitted out. Having, in effect, discounted other theories by this compliment, Lieutenant Mace wanted to be seen as a true open-minded expert. He returned to a possible weakness causing the fracture and subsequent sinking of the ship. He explained this might have happened over a period of time. The disaster that had befallen the *Ellan Vannin* could have happened to any ship. He did not feel that she had been damaged by a collision before she reached the Bar Lightship. If she had been, she would have signalled to the lightship that she required assistance. He did not think that a distress flare had been seen by the seaman on the Bar Lightship. What the seaman had seen was as a result of water rushing down the stoke-hole when the *Ellan Vannin* sank and expelling hot cinders and flames from the funnel. Furthermore, he said, the turning in of the plates had not been caused by a collision. He had performed an experiment before attending the enquiry which had proved this point. He had taken a metal tube and found that however he broke it some of the metal was turned inwards.

He concluded that a collision was not necessary to turn in the *Ellan Vannin*'s plates; this would have happened when the ship broke in two and sank. Lieutenant Mace explained that the location of the wreck, which was lying west by south, as opposed to the expected position which was more south by east, further supported his theory that the vessel had broached to before sinking.

THE ENQUIRY

The Steam Packet's barrister, Mr Bateson, immediately appreciated the significance of Lieutenant Mace's evidence and the impression he had made on the enquiry. The Steam Packet's theory of a collision had been shot to pieces by expert testimony from this experienced witness. Mr Bateson opened his cross-examination by coming straight to the point. He reminded the enquiry that Lieutenant Mace had given evidence at a previous inquest that the *Ellan Vannin* may have been in a collision. He wanted to know what had caused Lieutenant Mace to change his mind. If he could change his mind so quickly what was to say that his evidence today was of any more value?

Lieutenant Mace explained that yes, he would go so far as to say that the *Ellan Vannin* may have been in a collision, but, in his professional opinion, he did not think that she had been. Mr Bateson moved on to another possibility. Could the Ellan Vannin have collided with the Q1 buoy? Lieutenant Mace was dismissive of this. In his opinion the *Ellan Vannin* never even reached the Q1 buoy. He did not think the vessel got past where the wreck was now lying. He went on to remind Mr Bateson that the *Heroic* had pooped three times. The Ellan Vannin was going in a more southerly direction and was therefore more likely to poop and broach to. Further, the sea's effect would have been much greater on the *Ellan Vannin* as she was smaller than the *Heroic*.

The President intervened. He was startled to hear that a vessel could sink in circumstances where there had been no collision. Lieutenant Mace's response was simple: 'Lots of ships do sink solely because of adverse weather', he said. He went on to confirm that his stern-first sinking theory was consistent with the theory of mischief having started previously. An early indication that Lieutenant Mace's theory of why the *Ellan Vannin* sank was going to be adopted by the enquiry came when he finished his evidence. He was told that his theory and evidence were 'of great assistance to the enquiry'. The parties adjourned for lunch.

After the luncheon adjournment, Mr Millar was recalled to give evidence about the state of the plates that had been replaced when the *Ellan Vannin* bumped against a pier. Mr Millar was able to inform the enquiry that the plates had buckled and had not fractured. This information was significant as the plates could have been expected to have fractured if they had been brittle and had been weakened.

Mr Bateson followed the path laid down by all advocates. Finish your case on a high note with a good witness. He called Harry Roscoe, a member of the Institute of Naval Architects and Surveyors. Mr Roscoe was a naval architect of great experience and had designed ships for most of the Atlantic shipping companies. To call a witness of Mr Roscoe's calibre was another illustration that the Steam Packet were prepared to pay for the best technical assistance at the enquiry.

Mr Roscoe came straight to the point. He did not agree with Lieutenant Mace's theory that the *Ellan Vannin* sank stern first. If the *Ellan Vannin* had sunk stern first how did the cargo get through the bulkhead into the steerage part of the ship? The only way the cargo could have been in steerage was if the *Ellan Vannin*'s bow sank first.

He also rejected the idea of the *Ellan Vannin* striking the chain of the Q1 buoy. What had happened, in his opinion, was that floating wreckage had damaged the bottom of the *Ellan Vannin* and she had sunk. He referred, by way of examples, to the paddle steamers *Queen Victoria* and *Mona's Queen*. Both of these vessels had sustained serious damage to their paddle wheels as well as fractured plates when they had hit submerged wreckage.

Mr Roscoe's theory that the position of the cargo indicated that the *Ellan Vannin* had gone down bow first was soon itself in trouble when one of the divers, Mr Carter, was recalled. He was asked to provide evidence about the location of the cargo and he told the enquiry that it was not where Mr Roscoe had assumed it to be. On resuming his evidence Mr Roscoe agreed that the location of the cargo did not support his theory that the *Ellan Vannin* sank bow first, but he still believed that the vessel had come into contact with something, either on its bottom or its side, and had been holed. The forecastle or chain locker had filled with water, the ship then rose and fell, with the motion of the sea extending the break. The *Ellan Vannin*, so his theory went, then broached to, was struck by seas on the deck and went down. She broke into two parts when she got to the sea bed or in the process of sinking, though he believed that the

SUMMONS TO WITNESS.

SHIPPING CASUALTY.—Formal Investigation.
Merchant Shipping Act, 1894, sec. 466 (10).

In the City of Liverpool.

THE ENQUIRY

greater part of the fracture occurred after she struck the bottom.

As to Lieutenant Mace's suggestion that the *Ellan Vannin* had been weakened over time, Mr Roscoe kept to his brief to protect the Steam Packet's interests. He rejected the idea, claiming that a ship could become weakened over time only if it was flat-bottomed and repeatedly rested on the mud when the tide was out of the harbour. There would be no weakening of a ship such as the *Ellan Vannin* which didn't have a flat bottom.

He returned to what he thought had probably happened. The *Ellan Vannin* had come into contact with floating wreckage and this had caused her to sink. The sinking had happened very quickly, because there had been no time to launch the lifeboats properly or for any of the passengers or crew to don lifebelts.

After Mr Roscoe's evidence ended Mr Bateson recalled, as his final witness, Mr Blackburn, the Steam Packet's Superintendent Engineer. His evidence would have countered any thought that the Steam Packet had given up maintaining the *Ellan Vannin* because they had ordered a new ship. Certainly, a new vessel had been laid down in June 1909, but this was not intended to replace the *Ellan Vannin*. The ship that had been laid down was to replace the paddle steamer *Mona III* which had been disposed of in September 1909.

All the evidence had now been heard and it fell to Mr Bateson to display the skills of his craft in his closing speech to the enquiry: to persuade a fellow lawyer and three shipping assessors that the evidence that they had heard over three long days should not in any way be construed as amounting to a criticism of the Steam Packet.

Mr Bateson started by referring immediately to the issue that had arisen frequently throughout the enquiry: the age of the *Ellan Vannin*. He maintained that age was no detriment to the safety of an iron vessel if she was properly maintained. In support of this he referred to the highest authority, the noted expert Sir William White. Sir William, a naval architect, had designed numerous ships, including several battleships. Some of the *Ellan Vannin*'s plates had lasted nearly 50 years which showed their quality. Mr

Millar, the Board of Trade surveyor, had given evidence to the enquiry that he had watched to see that none of the ship's plates had wasted or corroded.

The *Ellan Vannin* was a popular boat, manned by an excellent crew and the enquiry would doubtless take into account the experience and qualifications of the captain and his officers. The ship belonged to a company whose reputation and business depended on safely carrying 800,000 passengers a year.

All of these factors provided a basis, maintained Mr Bateson, for the assumption that the sinking did not happen through want of care or because of the unfit condition of the ship's hull. As Master Kewley had said, the hurricane weather was the worst he'd ever seen. The enquiry had also heard further accounts of the appalling weather faced by Captain Teare. Witnesses had said that even if distress signals had been seen no one could have got close to the *Ellan Vannin* to rescue her passengers and crew because of the dreadful seas.

Mr Bateson returned to the possibility that the *Ellan Vannin* had been sunk by coming into contact with the Q1 buoy. He did not accept that this was the case. However, the reference to a collision did enable Mr Bateson to move swiftly onto the possibility of the *Ellan Vannin* colliding with a more substantial object. The Steam Packet's case, from first to last, was that there had been a collision, and this had caused the vessel to sink.

The Steam Packet did not accept the theory that the *Ellan Vannin* had sunk stern first. If this had been the case then it was difficult to account for the lack of bodies that had been found on the vessel. Further, if she had sunk stern first then there would have been time for some of the engine room staff and other crew and passengers to get on deck and escape, and the cargo would have been piled up aft, which it was not.

Mr Bateson suggested that the enquiry should be slow to accept the theory that having sunk stern first with the bow sticking out of the water, the air and sea had broken the bow off. If the bow had been out of the water, then the wooden deck would have been blown away before the iron sides. In the gale that was blowing at the time, the wreckage from the wooden

SUMMONS TO WITNESS.
SHIPPING CASUALTY.—Formal Investigation.
MERCHANT SHIPPING ACT, 1894, sec. 466 (10)

In the City of Liverpool.

THE ENQUIRY

deck would have broken into many pieces. However, some of the divers had given evidence that they could still walk across the deck. As for the theory that the *Ellan Vannin* had broached to, such a theory was difficult to accept because of the damage to the forward part of the ship.

Mr Bateson's prime responsibility was to ensure that there was no criticism whatsoever of the Steam Packet and he hammered home again the point that the enquiry should not come to findings against the owners of the ship. In order to criticise the Steam Packet the enquiry must have heard evidence that the Company was at fault. There had been no evidence of this sort, he claimed, though he did not refer to Lieutenant Mace's view that Captain Teare should not have crossed the Bar because of the state of the weather.

After Mr Bateson had finished his closing submission the enquiry gave some thought as to when they would announce their conclusions. This was not an easy case. As there were no witnesses or direct evidence as to the circumstances which caused the *Ellan Vannin* to sink, such evidence as there was would require careful consideration. The theories advanced before the enquiry needed much deliberation to see if one piece of evidence tipped the scales in favour of one theory rather than another. The enquiry's task could not be completed on that day. The enquiry therefore adjourned until the following Saturday, 12th March.

Many of the participants in the three days of the hearing returned to hear the enquiry's decision. Would the President, Mr Shepherd Little, be able to solve the mystery convincingly from the evidence submitted, and would he make critical findings of the condition of the ship, the captain and the crew? Despite the acknowledged difficulties the *Ellan Vannin* faced that night, the reputation of the Steam Packet Company could suffer a serious blow if such criticisms were made.

In the event, the enquiry found that the *Ellan Vannin* was in a good and seaworthy condition as regards its hull and equipment when she left Ramsey. Her cargo was properly stowed and secured from shifting, and the weight was distributed so as to make the vessel easy to handle in rough sea. She was not overloaded and was in good trim for a voyage to Liverpool. The *Ellan Vannin* encountered extraordinarily bad weather which caused her to broach to. The seas washed away the aft companion filling the aft part of the vessel, which caused her to sink by the stern leaving the bows out of the water. While in this position, the heavy seas striking the fore-part of the ship broke the bows away causing the wreckage to be in two parts. There was no evidence on which the enquiry could rely that suggested the *Ellan Vannin* had been in a collision either with another vessel or with submerged or floating wreckage.

To the Steam Packet's relief, the enquiry did not find that the breaking away of the ship's bow in these exceptional circumstances implied any structural weakness. The catastrophe by which the vessel was overtaken must have been so sudden that there was probably little or no time for those on board even to put on lifebelts or to take any other steps to save life. Sadly, all of those on board had drowned.

There was some acknowledgement of the Steam Packet's collision theory in the minority report of one of the shipping assessors, Captain Mitchell. He concluded that the *Ellan Vannin* broached to or had to be brought to against a heavy sea running on her starboard side. While in this position, for some unknown reason, the butt straps under the chain locker gave way. There was a strong inrush of water that filled the forward compartment, and finally all the butt straps on the ship's sides gave way causing the vessel to go down head first with little or no warning. This explanation was supported by the vessel being broken in two pieces from under the chain locker upwards. Any change of course by the *Ellan Vannin* would bring the full force of wind on her starboard bow. Captain Mitchell felt that possibly her port bow touched or collided with the Q1 buoy. Any collision between the *Ellan Vannin* and the Q1 buoy caused the buoy to break adrift on the morning of the disaster.

As the enquiry had been set up by the Board of Trade, it was for them to formally issue the official report. This was done in London on 8th April 1910. There were no substantial changes to the oral judgement delivered by the President. The full report is shown at Appendix II.

THE ENQUIRY

The Harbour Board must have been satisfied with the result. The Board's main fear, that there might have been a finding of unmarked wreckage, was specifically refuted. Similarly, the Steam Packet could be pleased with the results. There was no criticism of the Company. The enquiry might have been divided about which part of the *Ellan Vannin* sank first, but there was no doubting the enquiry's main conclusion: the *Ellan Vannin* had been sunk, not as the result of a collision or incompetent crewing, but because of the heavy seas.

SUMMONS TO WITNESS.

SHIPPING CASUALTY.—Formal Investigation.

Merchant Shipping Act, 1894, sec. 466 (10).

In the City of Liverpool.

THE ENQUIRY

REFER TO
C 843
IN YOUR REPLY

TELEGRAMS:
"ORFORDS, LIVERPOOL."

TELEPHONE 6228.

Thomas Orford & Son,
AGENTS
ISLE OF MAN STEAM PACKET COMPANY LIMITED.
(INCORPORATED IN THE ISLE OF MAN.)

YOUR
REFERENCE

17, Drury Buildings, 21, Water Street,
Liverpool, March 21st 1910

PASSENGERS, THEIR LUGGAGE LIVE STOCK, AND GOODS ONLY CONVEYED SUBJECT TO THE CONDITIONS OF CARRIAGE OF THE COMPANY AS EXHIBITED IN THEIR OFFICES AND ON BOARD THEIR STEAMERS.

Mr James Bell,
RAMSEY.

Dear Sir,

Can you inform us, for the information of the Board of Trade, how many pens were utilized (and their approximate position) for the sheep on the "ELLAN VANNIN" from Ramsey on her last voyage, and, if possible, give the approximate weight of them on either side.
A sketch of the fore part of the steamer shewing the pens, and the after line of the forecastle deck would be useful. Can you say how many sheep (if any) were penned outside the cover of the forecastle deck ?.

Yours truly

Thomas Orford & Son

P. S. Mr Blackburn informs us that there is a plan at Douglas shewing the position of the pens: a sketch from this might be taken and (presuming you know) be marked by you.

LETTER FROM THOMAS ORFORD'S SEEKING FURTHER DETAILS OF THE LOADING OF THE ELLAN VANNIN'S CARGO. FOR SOME REASON THE BOARD OF TRADE, SUBSEQUENT TO THE END OF THE ENQUIRY, STILL WANTED MORE INFORMATION.

CHAPTER NINE

THE ELLAN VANNIN DISASTER FUND

Raising funds in the aftermath of the *Ellan Vannin* disaster was an early example of decentralisation. Although there was a central committee presided over by the Lieutenant Governor and charged with overseeing the direction that the Fund should take, most of the actual work was delegated to individual districts. Most towns on the Island had a local committee which was responsible for fund raising activities in their area. There were also local fund raising committees in England, in particular in Lancashire and north-western towns including Liverpool, Manchester, Preston, Southport, Bolton, Barrow-in-Furness and Blackpool. Readers of the *Blackpool Times*, which circulated in Blackpool and Fleetwood, contributed £124.10s.

Not untypical of the local committees on the Island was that in Douglas. The chairman was the Mayor, and the Town Clerk acted as secretary. Supporting these gentlemen was an executive committee. Indeed, such were the efforts to raise funds that Douglas was divided into 50 districts for the purposes of street collections. Collecting books

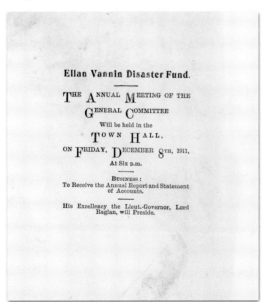

NOTICE FOR THE 1911 AGM OF THE ELLAN VANNIN DISASTER FUND.

'...And now abideth faith, hope, charity, these three; but the greatest of these is charity'
The Bible.

were printed and issued. The Town Clerk wanted more than just the people of Douglas to contribute. He wrote to all major shipping lines asking for contributions. He also circulated a letter to many prominent people and organisations in England, advising them of the Fund. These initiatives were, no doubt, partly responsible for contributions coming in from all over the United Kingdom.

All of the Island was involved as well as other parts of the world where there was an affinity to the Manx nation and the plight of those who lost someone on the *Ellan Vannin*. One of the most prominent efforts was in the Transvaal. At a meeting in Johannesburg on 8th January 1910, the Manx Association unanimously resolved to start an *Ellan Vannin* fund.

In addition to specific events there were many *ad hoc* collections held and other activities to which there was always a very generous response. Fund raising started almost immediately after the disaster and many of the events that were held were typical social activities of the early part of the 20th Century. A well supported concert was held at Kelly's Theatre in Liverpool. The owner provided the theatre free and artists from Liverpool, Birkenhead and Manchester provided their acts without charge. Mr Derwent Hall Caine travelled from London especially to read his father's poem, 'Charlie, the Manx Cox'. His father was unable to attend as he was on the continent. Hall Caine was later criticised on the Isle of Man for failing to give any money to the fund, though in fact he was at the top of the list of contributers to the Disaster Fund set up by the *Daily Telegraph* at his instigation. The proprietors of the newspaper themselves gave £10.

A notable absentee at the concert was Miss Marie Lloyd. The famous performer, who had been due to attend, was prevented by illness. She sent a contribution of five guineas. Among the distinguished visitors were the Lord Mayors and Lady Mayoresses of Liverpool and Bootle.

Liverpool staged another major concert at St. George's Hall where various artists performed, including the Liverpool Constabulary Band. Nearly 2,000 people attended. The Liverpool Manx Society also held a concert, as did the Star Theatre.

**THE PENDANT MADE FROM A SIXPENCE TAKEN FROM
THE PAY PACKET OF CREWMAN JOHN COOK**

THE ELLAN VANNIN DISASTER FUND

Concerts were held in various Lancashire towns as well, for example, at the Winter Gardens in Southport. Apparently, some 22 years before the *Ellan Vannin* was lost, 20 members of the Southport lifeboat crew had been drowned trying to rescue the German barque, *Mexico*. The Isle of Man had assisted in Southport's fund raising activities. Although they were parted by the sea, the town felt united in sympathy with the Isle of Man and wished to help the dependants of those lost on the *Ellan Vannin*. Over £200 was raised by the concert.

One concert was actually held on board ship. The SS *Karina* was an Elder Dempster line ship which had left Liverpool on 1st December 1909 and experienced the gale through which the *Ellan Vannin* sailed. On New Year's eve the *Karina* was anchored near Calabar on the West African coast. The stewards' concert raised £2.10 shillings. A cheque for this sum was sent to the Mayor of Douglas when the *Karina* arrived back in port at the end of January 1910.

Many concerts were held on the Isle of Man to raise funds. One of the largest was at the Gaiety Theatre in Douglas. Local traders and businesses wished to play their part in helping the fund and the theatre was provided without charge. The printing of tickets and posters was charged at a reduced rate to ensure that as much of the money as possible went to the Fund. The Lieutenant Governor and his wife were in attendance. The performers included the Manx Choir, the Douglas Male Choristers and the Douglas Philharmonic Orchestra. For many, the most emotional moment of the whole concert was a reading of the poem *The Wreck of the Ellan Vannin* by Fred Buxton. This moving poem was regularly recited at fund raising events and brought tears to many peoples' eyes when it was read at a concert at Buxton's Pavilion in Douglas. Copies of the poem were in great demand. It was printed on special cards in two editions and sales raised £3.7s.0d.

Many other poems about the *Ellan Vannin* were written. One such was by a Mr Gell. His poem was printed on cards which were suitable for framing, and sales were another valuable source of income to the Fund.

The Douglas Male Choristers were very prominent in raising funds after the disaster. It may be that a member of the crew or one of the passengers lost on the *Ellan Vannin* was a chorister, although there is no record of this. In any event, the choristers gave concerts in Peel, Castletown and Port St. Mary, as well as in Liverpool, Manchester and Bolton. The committee of the Choristers was pleased to report that employers had agreed to let their workers be absent from work so they could take part in the three concerts in England.

A notable feature of the Manchester concert on 12th January 1910 at the Free Trade Hall was the lavish programme. The cover illustrated ships' distress and shore flags, as well as storm warning cones. Inside were views of Douglas and other parts of the Island and portraits of all those lost on the *Ellan Vannin*. The Lord Mayor and Lady Mayoress of Manchester were present to hear numerous encores by the Choristers. Mancunians wanted the Douglas Choir to return to give another concert when the disaster was not on everyone's mind.

Invariably, the Island concerts involved local choral and musical groups as in Peel, where the Peel Choral Society held a concert. News of the Steam Packet's legal liability for the loss may have added momentum to fund raising efforts. The *Ellan Vannin* was registered in Douglas. The Workmens Compensation Act only applied to United Kingdom registered ships and so the Steam Packet were not therefore liable to compensate the widows and children of the crew. However, as we have seen, the Company was more than generous in its treatment of the crews' dependants.

In addition to the concerts which raised large amounts for the Fund, a variety of other activities took place. In the run up to Christmas, cake sales throughout the Island and Lancashire were a popular way to support the *Ellan Vannin* Fund. Events were held all over the north-west of England. For example Gouldens, a furrier in Blackpool, held a whist drive, the proceeds of which went to the Fund. Various masonic lodges also held whist drives. Numerous football matches were organised.

THE ELLAN VANNIN DISASTER FUND

On the Island, the Palace Hockey Club held a gymkhana, including a bun and ginger beer race, which involved skating around the ring and eating and drinking. Although there was a prize for the winners of the race, the winners gave their prize money to the Fund. Monies were also raised from those attending a hockey match at Pulrose cricket ground in Douglas. All of these activities played their part in adding to the growing size of the Fund.

The Lieutenant Governor's wife, Lady Raglan, decided that she would hold an exchange and mart at Government House for the children of those lost on the *Ellan Vannin*. The event took place at Christmas and those invited were asked to bring half a pound of any article to sell, and at the same time to buy a half a pound of items that had been brought by others. The funds raised by this event enabled each child to have 10 shillings placed in a Post Office Savings Bank account. Her Ladyship wished to encourage the valuable habit of thrift. However, of more immediate appeal to the children who had lost their fathers or mothers was a Christmas party held at Government House.

One of the most impressive Douglas events was when Mr Noah Moore's Choir led a procession of hymn singers. Two bands, the Douglas Volunteer and Town Band, followed behind. The procession ended at a mass service at the Palace on the sea front. Children marched from various Sunday schools to attend. The Douglas Male Choristers led the congregation in singing at the service. There were street collectors on the route of the procession.

Day after day the newspapers recorded personal and corporate and other contributions to the Fund. Many people did not wish the amount they contributed to be disclosed, and this was respected by the newspapers which printed the lists of contributors. Similarly, some donors wished to remain completely anonymous. One of the notable features of the Fund was that many people made more than one donation as the horror of the tragedy became more and more apparent to those on the Island and elsewhere.

Indeed, it is hard to find any section of Island society, be they advocates, captains of parishes, aldermen and councillors, other groups of professionals, children, clubs and societies who did not contribute. Many vicars, as well as ensuring that their churches contributed, also contributed personally. The Manx Labour Party, at a meeting to discuss old age pensions, collected 11s.6d.

Numerous of the Island's schools made contributions to the Fund. There were also collections that were organised by the heads of schools in Birkenhead and elsewhere on Merseyside.

Collections were taken at many places of work and groups of workers across the Island as well as in England contributed generously. The Steam Packet's staff and agents made contributions, and collections were held at football matches involving Liverpool and Everton at Anfield and Goodison Park respectively.

Many donations came from people with fond memories of holidaying in the Island, and Manxmen abroad also played their part. For example, one contribution was from 'Manx Citizens in the USA', and a large contribution came from Bisbee, Arizona. This relatively small community sent $104.75c. There were other contributions from Manx societies in the colonies of Africa and the East.

The local committees took all possible steps to ensure that everyone who might wish to make a contribution was aware of how this could be done. Letters were written to the editors of all the newspapers in the north-west of England asking them to alert their readers to the existence of the Fund.

In addition to donations from individuals and organisations, there were numerous Sunday schools, societies, social clubs and similar that held collections for the Fund. There was assistance from such bodies as The Provincial Grand Black Royal Arch Chapter of England, and The Laundry and Domestic Appliances Exhibition Syndicate, which contributed £6.7s.6d. The Syndicate had twice hired the *Ellan Vannin* in 1909 to convey their Exhibition to and from Douglas. The contribution was made because of the kindness and attention of the crew on those journeys.

Inevitably, some took advantage of the fund-raising and there were reported warnings of bogus collectors. However, such fears were soon dispelled

THE ELLAN VANNIN DISASTER FUND

and money continued to flood in. In the early days there had been some slight resistance to contributing to the Fund because it was thought that only the crew's dependants would benefit. It was soon made clear, however, that the needy dependants of both crew and passengers would benefit.

By the spring of 1910, approximately three months after the disaster, a total of £12,997.6s.3d was held by the Fund. As we have seen, the Steam Packet contributed £1,000, and the largest donations from companies were of approximately £100.

Today's equivalent of £12,997.6s.3d has been estimated by Martin Caley of the Economic Affairs Division of the Isle of Man Government as having a value of nearly £922,000. The size of the total is a reflection of the effect the disaster had on the Island, and a tribute to the efforts of all those involved with the Fund.

There is little record of any life assurance policies held by passengers. There is only one report in a newspaper that one of the passengers had taken a policy with the Yorkshire Insurance Company a few days before the *Ellan Vannin* sank, and that the policy monies were therefore now due. However, it will be recalled that Captain Teare had a £200 policy. Some other crew members had friendly society policies for £10 or £15.

Concern was frequently expressed that the Fund should be properly administered. There were many previous examples of funds where widows and children had been left starving, whilst monies were distributed to people who were not intended to benefit. The proper investment of the Fund was also important. Problems with the fund collected after the sinking of the naval ships *Tiger* and *Gladiator* two years previously was referred to. This fund totalled £9,860. £9,000 was invested with Portsmouth Corporation for 25 years. When the needs were greatest, in the early years of the fund, there was very little available to be distributed; the majority of the capital was tied up for 25 years!

One of the Trustees' first tasks was to appoint an actuary to devise a scheme of distribution as well as to recommend how to invest the money. The actuary could also regularly advise on the Fund's solvency and whether the benefits could be increased. The Royal Insurance Company, (now the Royal & Sun Alliance), whose head office was in Liverpool, already had extensive Isle of Man connections. The Royal's actuary, Mr Duncan C Fraser, and later his office, were to be the Fund's honorary actuary for nearly 50 years. Although he was based in Liverpool, Mr Fraser took his duties seriously and regularly crossed to the Island to present his annual report.

Mr Fraser drew up a scheme that would eventually exhaust the Fund. The Fund was designed to provide a benefit for widows for life or until remarriage and for children until sixteen. The amount of the benefit was to be dependent on all the circumstances of each case, especially the earning power of each beneficiary. There should be no cast iron rules. There was a need to be pragmatic. The expected interest of the Fund's investments was 3½% per annum.

The Fund also benefited from the accountancy services of W H Walker and Co., now Pannell Kerr Forster, the Douglas accountants, who acted as honorary auditors of the Fund.

The principal investments of the Fund were as follows:

Corporation of Douglas £3,500 Bonds 3½%
Corporation of Liverpool £3,500 Bonds 3½%
Laxey Village Commissioners £4,000 Bonds 4%

In the days of the Ellan Vannin Fund, inflation was low and there were certain restrictions on trust funds investing other than in government, or in this case, local authority securities. The Fund does not appear at any stage to have been invested in equities. The Fund made weekly allowances of variable amounts to all of those who were in need of assistance. These payments were often made quarterly in an attempt to avoid administrative costs.

All of the families of the crew received assistance from the Fund and five families of passengers benefited from the Fund. The following passengers' families were the principal beneficiaries: Miss Fisher, Messrs Higginbotham, Williams, Blevin and Quayle. Limited assistance was given to Miss Findlay's family. A total of £15 was to be paid in

THE ELLAN VANNIN DISASTER FUND

weekly instalments until the sum was used up. The assistance to Mr Blevin's family, which incidentally continued for 50 years, might appear surprising. When probate was granted to his widow Mr Blevin's net estate was very sizeable, £2,166.

The family of one of the passengers, Mr Newall, made no claim on the Fund but were awarded an ex-gratia payment of £10. The family of Mr and Mrs Heaton Johnson, two other passengers, also made no claim. Indeed, the family was most upset by incorrect rumours that Mr Heaton Johnson had made no provision for his three children. In fact the family were anxious for the Fund's trustees to know they would not be making a claim as the children's father had made ample provision for them.

The original amounts awarded, and the circumstances that led to the Trustees deciding on an increase, or at times a reduction in the weekly amount paid, provide a fascinating insight into the period during which the Fund operated. There were frequent references to widows' abilities to keep boarding houses, illustrating the dominant position of the Island's tourist business at that time. Many of the possible occupations that widows could follow no longer exist, for example, taking in washing. The conditions in which families lived illustrated the harsh times, such as a widow and five children living in one room in Barrack Street, Douglas. Diseases, since confined to history, were frequently referred to, such as consumption (tuberculosis). A final commentary on the times is given by the observation in respect of the family of Mr Kinley, the second mate. The family were said to be 'very respectable people' and therefore unlikely to apply for assistance. The time when it was thought to be unrespectable to seek assistance did not end until many years after the *Ellan Vannin* sank.

The Fund continued uneventfully throughout peace and two world wars until its objectives had been fulfilled. Occasionally, the actuary would advise there was an expected shortfall in the Fund, often of relatively small sums, £50 or £100 or so. The Steam Packet made contributions of this size throughout the lifetime of the Fund. Thanks to these contributions the Fund's solvency was maintained. In later years, on

a number of occasions, winding up the Fund and purchasing annuities for the remaining beneficiaries was considered, but no action was taken.

After nearly 50 years all but one of the children of those lost on the *Ellan Vannin* were no longer receiving assistance, and many of the widows had died. The time had perhaps come to wind up the Fund. At the Trustees' meeting on 14th April 1959, the Lieutenant Governor, Sir Ambrose Flux Dundas, formally raised the question of whether the Fund should be brought to a conclusion. As in the beginning, in 1909, the Trustees included the Lieutenant Governor and the Mayors of Douglas and Liverpool. However, at the start of the Fund's life there were 91 beneficiaries: 23 widows or widowers, 58 children and 10 others (parents, brothers and sisters that in some way were dependent on one of those lost). In April 1959 there were only three beneficiaries. They were Mrs Annie Crowley (a widow of one of the crew), aged 85, who lived in Cumberland and who was still receiving 14s.6d per week; Mrs F C Blevin (a widow of one of the passengers), aged 79, who lived in Cheltenham and was receiving 12s.6d per week and Miss Annie Benson (daughter of one of the crew), aged 69, who presumably lived in Ramsey because payments were made to Martins Bank's Ramsey branch, and who was receiving 5/- per week.

The Trustees wished to hand over to the Steam Packet the £700 left in the Fund. In turn, the Company agreed to accept responsibility for continuing to make payments. Should there be any residue when the last beneficiary died, this would belong to the Steam Packet. The residue was in consideration for the 'top-ups' and the cost of taking over the Trustees' responsibilities.

The Ellan Vannin Fund came to and end with the winding up declaration executed by the Trustees and the Steam Packet shortly after 14th April 1959. After nearly 50 years and 456 pages of minutes, there was to be no further public record of the payments to the last three beneficiaries. Details of these were, presumably, a minor sub-heading in the Steam Packet's million pound expenditure accounts.

The final public accounts of the Fund show

THE ELLAN VANNIN DISASTER FUND

half a century of prudent management. The Trustees had been pragmatic in distributing the money. Although cautious when necessary, there had been no undue caution which might have led to a build-up of money and a final profligate distribution to those who did not really need assistance when the Fund was wound up.

The last beneficiary of the Fund was Miss Annie Benson who was 20 in 1909 and in poor health. It was most unlikely that she would have been the last beneficiary, but she survived to the age of 85 before dying in 1974.

Total Receipts	£.s.d	Total Payments	£.s.d
Receipts and donations	£13,664.2.3	Amount paid in relief	£21,245.10.6
Bank and other interest on investments	£9,244.19.9	Expenses	£956.14.7
Investments repaid	£12,300.0.0	Investments made	£13,000.0.0
		Cash at bank	£6.16.11
	£35,209.2.0		£35,209.2.0

THE FINAL STATEMENT OF ACCOUNTS WHEN THE FUND WAS HANDED OVER TO THE STEAM PACKET IN 1959.

THE ELLAN VANNIN DISASTER FUND

Set out below is a representative selection of those who contributed to the Ellan Vannin Disaster Fund. Those persons and organisations shown illustrate the wide circle who were moved by the *Ellan Vannin* disaster. As noted earlier, many people did not wish the amount they contributed to be disclosed, and this was respected by newspapers which printed the lists of contributors.

The Salisbury Dancing Academy 16s

The shipbuilders Cammell Laird and Co. Ltd.,
      who had and were to build many ships for the Steam Packet £52.10s

His Worship the Lord Mayor of Douglas and the Lady Mayoress, Mrs Marsden ....10 guineas each

The Clerk of Rolls of the Isle of Man £10

The masters of Birkenhead Higher Elementary School £1.17s.6d

The Vicar General of the Isle of Man £20

The staff of the *Isle of Man Examiner* £5.5s

Heron & Brearley Ltd., one of the Island's brewers £105

Messrs Boots the Chemists £10.10s

The Isle of Man Mineral Water Manufacturers' Association £2.2s

Deemsters Callow and Moore ....£5 each

The Douglas Rocket Corp.; a crew member belonged to the Corp. £3

The Freemasons of Tynwald Lodge £25

King William's College, Castletown £8.6s.10d

The resident staff of Nobles's Hospital, Douglas £1.11s

The drawing office staff at Douglas Town Hall 10s.6d

The Isle of Man Licensed Victuallers' Association £21

Two permanent residents at the Douglas Bay Hotel 10s.6d

A permanent resident at the Sefton Hotel (believed to be Walter Keig) 5s

The Guinness Brewery from Dublin £10

The Directors of the Douglas Marine Drive Transport Co. Ltd. £10

The staff at Parr's Bank, Manchester ....

The Isle of Man Railway Co. £52.10s

Murrays Road School, Douglas - Saturday pocket money collection £3.17s.6d

Collection on board the Steam Packet's *Tynwald* £1.1s

The RNLI, Liverpool ....

The Dowager, Lady Loch, wife of a former Lieutenant Governor ....

Dentists from Manchester and Preston ....

The Isle of Man Board and Lodging Houses Proprietors' Association £5.5s

The Liverpool Manx Society ....

The Liverpool & North Wales Steamship Co.,
      which might in other times be considered a rival of the Steam Packet £25

Jas Lay & Co. Ltd., outfitters, Parliament Street, Ramsey £10

Okell & Son of the Falcon Brewery, Douglas £10.10s

THE ELLAN VANNIN DISASTER FUND

THE WRECK of the ELLAN VANNIN: Foundered in the Mersey, December 3rd, 1909.

SHE sailed away from Ramsey Bay,
    On a dark and cheerless morn:
The good ship Ellan Vannin,
    Monarch of many a storm.
The pride of Mona's noble fleet,
    The mother of them all.
For fifty years our little craft
    Had answered to the call.
A stouter boat, a sturdier crew,
    Ne'er fought the angry main.
We little thought it then, God knows!
    We'd see her not again.
My story hangs near Christmas time,
    And the Christ Child's holy birth;
And the message of love from the Father above,
    Of peace and goodwill on earth.
And the Vannin's crew, and the passengers, too,
    Maybe, would be thinking, as well,
Of the happy times and the Christmas chimes,
    And the singing of glad No'el.
'Tis time to sail! Friends bid farewell,
    The last goodbye is said,
And man and boat will be soon afloat
    On the ocean's mighty bed.
Clang! Goes the bell. The engines throb:
    "Now then, my lads, stand clear!"
'Tis the skipper's voice, from the bridge above -
    The gallant Captain Teare.
"Cast off those ropes! Go easy, there!"
    And the Vannin glides away,
Out in the gloom and the angry boom,
    Across the storm-swept bay.
See how she dips! See how she rides!
    And now to sight she's lost!
Eternal Father, strong to save,
    Watch o'er the tempest-tossed!
On, on, they go, and farther on,
    The cyclone fiercer grew;
But naught of fear is lurking here -
    A grim, determined crew.
There's Craine and Kinley, worthy mates,
    And seamen Clague and Cook,
And others, too, all brave and true,
    In deed, and word, and look.
Black gloom around, a dirty sea,
    None worse for years, 'tis said,
Can men and craft steer safely through
    The seething shoals ahead?
Aye! Aye!! we'll win, we've won before;
    Please God, we'll win again!

And the fighting ship, with roll and dip,
    Plunged o'er the surging main.
Howl! Howl! Ye waves, and snap your jaws,
    Lay wait to claim your prey;
But have a care! You shall not dare
    Make food of us to-day.
And so the good barque battles on,
    Dark night for dawn, is passed,
When lo! A shout from the keen look-out:
    The Mersey Bar! at last!
That dreaded Bar! once o'er the mark,
    And haven sure we'll find;
Once through those portals and we leave
    The danger zone behind.
Right well brave "Vannin" struggles on,
    Her timbers crack and strain,
And, answering grand to her pilot's hand,
    The Bar is passed again.
Thank God! thank God! A minute more,
    And safe we'll be and sound -
But what is that! a deafening crash,
    Black death waves surging round.
Great Heaven above! we're going down,
    Help! - mother! sister! wife!
To die like this, what dark despair!
    How frail a thing is life!
The cruel waves engulf their prey,
    The Rest! - behind a veil;
What's hidden there we ne'er can know,
    None live to tell the tale.
Out on the Quay, with anxious eye,
    Men watch, and fear, and wait.
Boat's overdue a long time now,
    Where is she? what's her fate?
Hush! what say you? a mail bag found,
    And life belts floating, too!
Alas! She's gone - no more we'll look
    On passengers or crew!
No more brave Ellan Vannin's bows
    On angry storm will ride;
She's paid the toll - full measure too! -
    The "Little Island's" pride.
Poor mourners left, of hope bereft,
    Pray God, on bended knee,
That He will save the souls who brave
    The perils of the sea.

FRED J. BUXTON.
Falcon Cliff Cottage, Douglas.

AFTER THE DISASTER NUMEROUS POEMS WERE WRITTEN, AND THIS ONE, BY FRED BUXTON, WAS READ AT MANY EVENTS HELD TO RAISE FUNDS FOR THE DEPENDANTS OF THOSE LOST.
IT WAS DEDICATED WITH DEEPEST SYMPATHY TO THE CHAIRMAN, DALRYMPLE MAITLAND, DIRECTORS I.O.M. STEAM PACKET CO., AND WIDOWS, ORPHANS, RELATIVES AND FRIENDS.

CHAPTER TEN
POSTSCRIPT

Chris Michael is a diver and member of the Liverpool University sub-aqua club. He and his colleagues have made many dives to seek out the remains of the *Ellan Vannin*. He has made his searches with a magnetometer and found a weak signal indicating the presence of ferrous metal. Although he

A SUPERB MODEL OF THE SS ELLAN VANNIN MADE BY DOUGLAS MODEL BUILDER PHIL WALKER. IT WAS COMMISSIONED BY CASTLETOWN RESIDENT TOM GLASSEY WHO ALSO WROTE AND RECORDED A SONG TO COMMEMORATE THE 90TH ANNIVERSARY OF THE LOSS.

has not obtained any echo sounder signal indicating that there is any material above the sea bed, the Kingfisher chart (as used by fishermen) shows one "fastener" (something a fishing net could snag on) nearby, though whether this is from the *Ellan Vannin* is not known. Underwater visibility is poor, though diving is feasible since the location is quite shallow which would allow any wreckage to be seen, but Chris Michael thinks that, in all probability, whatever

'Long may we sorrow for the ship that's lost,
Long may we sorrow for the tears she cost,
But sorrow breaks in joy for those that crossed.'

'The Sorrowful Crossing' by Cushag

remains of the *Ellan Vannin* is now completely covered in sand and silt.

A detailed examination of the *Ellan Vannin*, especially the hull, which may have provided some more clues as to why she sank, is obviously not now possible. Was the enquiry's report correct; did she sink because of the appaling weather? Or did she sink after a collision with a larger ship? Was there an attempt to launch the lifeboats? The davits were swung out, and only three passengers bodies were found on board; it might have been that there was time for people to assemble on deck, but that at the last moment they, and the ship, were overwhelmed by the sea.

Despite all the pages of speculation and the public enquiry, all of these questions and many more remain unanswered, and therefore ultimately, why the *Ellan Vannin* sank must remain a mystery.

However, public attention changed from the details of those involved, to the disaster generally and consequently we know very little of what happened to the widows and children of those lost. The direct Ramsey to Liverpool service no longer exists but the Steam Packet's route from Douglas to Liverpool remained the core of the Company's business until the mid 1980s. The disaster did not seem to affect total passenger numbers which increased on an annual basis, and in 1913 the company carried just on a million passengers. In the United Kingdom, after the Board of Trade enquiry report was published, apart from a couple of questions in the House of Commons concerning the age of passenger carrying ferries, little else was heard of the *Ellan Vannin*. But on the Island, few forgot the disaster which has become part of the Manx heritage. Over

POSTSCRIPT

HUGHIE JONES WHO WROTE THE SONG 'THE ELLAN VANNIN TRAGEDY' WHICH HAS BECOME A CLASSIC. IT WAS MADE FAMOUS BY THE LIVERPOOL FOLK GROUP 'THE SPINNERS' OF WHICH HUGHIE WAS A MEMBER.

the years there have been frequent references to the sinking. As anniversaries passed the *Ellan Vannin* was the subject of special features commemorating the disaster in newspapers, magazines and on the radio.

THE UNVEILING OF THE ELLAN VANNIN MEMORIAL PLAQUE ON RAMSEY QUAYSIDE ON 3RD DECEMBER, 1999. LEFT TO RIGHT: HON. TONY BROWN, MINISTER FOR PORTS; CHARLES GUARD, ADMINISTRATOR MANX HERITAGE FOUNDATION; GEOFF CORKISH, STEAM PACKET COMPANY; HON. NOEL CRINLGLE SHK, CHAIRMAN, MANX HERITAGE FOUNDATION.

Many poems and songs have been written about the loss, the most famous of which is *The Ellan Vannin Tragedy* by Hughie Jones of the Liverpool folkgroup *The Spinners*. This song has been sung in many a folk club, and was included in the second volume of *The Manx National Song Book*, published in 1979.

Many paintings, drawings and models of the boat have been made over the years and even today, one hundred years after the disaster, there are still Manx households which display a copy of the poster printed in 1909 by the *Isle of Man Examiner* which had as many photographs of the crew and passengers as could be obtained in the days after the sinking.

The Steam Packet was always conscious of the safety that it owed to the millions of passengers that it carried. The telegram announcing the loss of the *Ellan Vannin* remains on the office wall of a senior manager at the Company's head office in Imperial Buildings, Douglas. There are Steam Packet captains even today, although they will rarely admit it, that in making a decision whether to sail or not, have the fate of Captain Teare in the forefront of their minds, and no other Steam Packet ship has borne the name *Ellan Vannin*.

To mark the 90th anniversary of the sinking, the Manx Heritage Foundation placed a plaque on Ramsey quayside next to the berth that had been regularly used by the *Ellan Vannin*. A short service of remembrance was held on 3rd December 1999 attended by several descendents of those who had died.

During the centenary year of 2009, Isle of Man Post issued a set of stamps, designed by Peter Hearsey, to commemorate the event.

A MINIATURE SHEET FROM THE SERIES OF STAMPS ISSUED BY ISLE OF MAN POST TO COMMEMORATE THE CENTENARY OF THE SINKING OF THE ELLAN VANNIN.

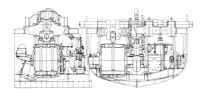

APPENDIX I

SS ELLAN VANNIN - FOR THE EXPERTS

Although Fred Henry's book on Steam Packet vessels suggests *Mona's Isle II* had paddle side lever machinery, the better opinion appears to be that *Mona's Isle II* was the first of the Company's steamers to be fitted with simple oscillating engines. This type of engine possessed a number of advantages over the side lever engine which had been so favoured by Napier and had been previously used by the Company.

Oscillating engines took up much less space and had fewer working parts. The chief feature being the connecting rod was dispensed with. The upper end of the piston rod was fitted with a bearing and worked directly on the crankpin. The cylinder was placed vertically under the crankshaft and was carried on two trunnions near the middle of its length so that it could freely sway to and fro through a small arc, and thus permit the piston rod to follow the movements of the

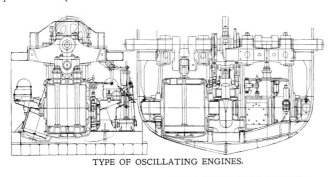

TYPE OF OSCILLATING ENGINES.

TYPE OF OSCILLATING ENGINES.

crank. Marine engineers will pay tribute to the advantages, in terms of reliability, of oscillating engines and their place in the development of steamers throughout the world. The twin cylinder oscillating machinery (44" - 48") of the *Mona's Isle II* had a N.H.P. (nominal horse power) of 130. The I.H.P. (indicated horse power) was 600.

She was re-boilered and converted to twin screw by the fitting of two inverted compound surface condensing engines and the new engines each had two cylinders (diameter 18" and 34" with a stroke of 24") which had a N.H.P. and I.H.P. of 100 and 500 respectively. The boilers which had a raised pressure of 80lb p.s.i. (per square inch) and other conversion works cost

nearly £9000.

Her last Lloyd's registration number was 405. She was not classed in Lloyd's Register Book.

The builders' plans and the plans used for the *Ellan Vannin*'s later conversion were probably thrown away after the works were completed. Unfortunately it would therefore seem that no plans of the *Mona's Isle II* or the *Ellan Vannin* remain. It is not therefore possible to describe with absolute accuracy the specifications of the *Ellan Vannin*. The following details are derived from what information is available. Many of the details come from official sources and can therefore be relied on as an accurate description of the *Ellan Vannin* at the time of her last voyage.

The *Ellan Vannin* was a schooner rigged, two masted, single bottomed, one deck vessel. She had four iron bulkheads, two water ballast tanks, one at each end of the vessel which had a total capacity of 44 tons. She had a raised quarter deck, with a house on the after part and a bridge amidships with a wheel house thereon from where she was steered by hand, as she did not have a steam steering gear.

She had a top-gallant forecastle under which was the steerage. Forward of the steerage was the forecastle, and under the forecastle, the chain locker, and abaft the chain locker, one of the water ballast tanks. Between these compartments and the forehold there was an iron bulkhead. She had two cargo holds. The fore hatchway measured 15 feet by 6 feet 10 inches. The height of the coamings (the raised lip with which openings in the upper deck such as hatchways below, are framed to prevent water running down the openings into the space below) was 15 inches. The after hatchway measured 12 feet by 6 feet 4 inches also with coamings of 15 inches height.

The height of the engine room skylight above the bridge deck was 3 feet 2 inches, and from the main deck to the bridge deck 7 feet 4 inches, the length being 9 feet.

Her bulwarks were 4 feet 6 inches in height, with two freeing ports, one on each side, measuring 14 inches by 9 inches, and two others, one on each side, measuring 24 inches by 24 inches. She had three deck

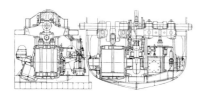

hand pumps in connection with the bilges. The depth in the hold from the tonnage deck to the ceiling at midships was 10 feet 7 inches. She carried two lifeboats under their own davits (the pair of cranes that are used for hoisting and lowering the lifeboat) with the necessary equipment. They rested on chocks on the bridge amidships. Photographic evidence suggested it would be easy to get the lifeboats out. The aggregate capacity of the lifeboats was 382 cubic feet, and they were capable of accommodating 38 persons. There were also on board 320 lifebelts and six lifebuoys.

Differing details of the net and gross tonnage are given in the various books on the Company's vessels. The Confidential Index held by Lloyd's of London which was for the use of underwriters and marine insurance companies that subscribed to Lloyd's

gave the vessel's original net and gross tonnages as 152 and 342 tons respectively. The net figure was reported as being reduced to 97 tons in 1886 although the gross tonnage remained at 342 tons. In 1890 there was an increase to 123 tons net and 374 tons gross. A further increase followed in 1895 to 128 tons net and 380 tons gross. The 1910 Board of Trade enquiry gave the *Ellan Vannin*'s net tonnage as 128.30 tons with a gross tonnage of 379.53 tons. The difference between net and gross tonnage should perhaps be mentioned for those unfamiliar with the terms. Gross tonnage, which is used for registration and insurance purposes, is calculated as the internal capacity of the vessel. Net tonnage, which is used for harbour dues, is the gross tonnage less space that cannot be used for cargo, for example, the space occupied by the engines.

The Steam Packet Fleet in 1909

Fleet Number	Name	Date launched or acquired by Steam Packet	Details	Gross Tonnage	Max Speed in Knots
9	Ellan Vannin	10/4/1860	Iron Twin Screw Steamer	380	13
13	King Orry II	27/3/1871	Iron Paddle Steamer	1104	17
17	Fenella I	9/6/1881	Iron Twin Screw Steamer	564	$13^1/_2$
18	Mona's Isle III	16/5/1882	Steel Paddle Steamer	1564	$17^1/_2$
20	Mona's Queen II	18/4/1885	Steel Paddle Steamer	1559	18
21	Queen Victoria	23/11/1888	Steel Paddle Steamer	1657	$20^1/_2$
22	Prince of Wales	23/11/1888	Steel Paddle Steamer	1657	$20^1/_2$
23	Tynwald III	11/5/1891	Steel Twin Screw Steamer	937	18
24	Empress Queen	4/3/1897	Steel Paddle Steamer	2140	$21^1/_2$
25	Douglas III	2/3/1889	Steel Single Screw Steamer	813	15
26	Mona III	July 1903	Steel Paddle Steamer	1212	18
27	Viking	7/3/1905	Steel Triple Screw Turbine Steamer	1957	23
28	Ben-my-Chree III	24/3/1908	Steel Triple Screw Turbine Steamer	2651	$24^1/_2$

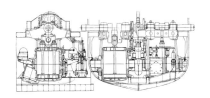

APPENDIX I

SS ELLAN VANNIN - FOR THE EXPERTS

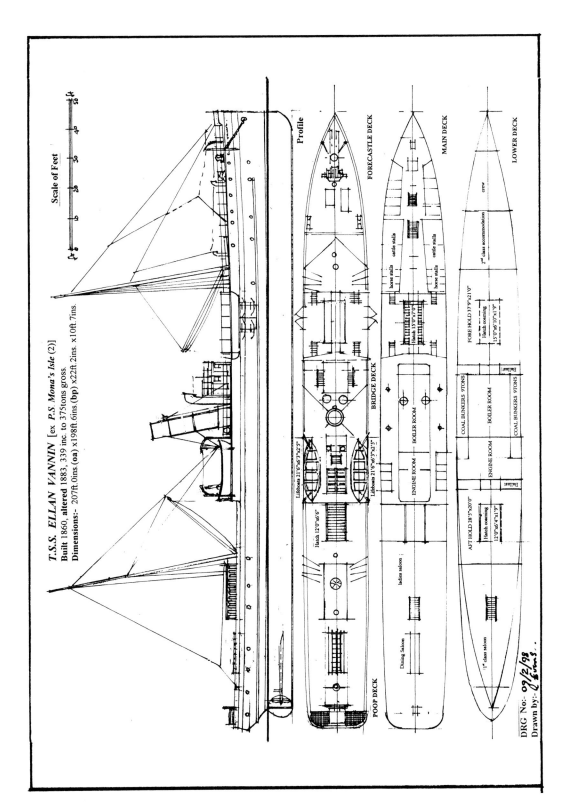

Scale of Feet

Profile

FORECASTLE DECK

MAIN DECK

LOWER DECK

BRIDGE DECK

POOP DECK

T.S.S. ELLAN VANNIN [ex *P.S. Mona's Isle* (2)]
Built 1860, altered 1883, 339 inc. to 375tons gross.
Dimensions:- 207ft.0ins.(oa) x198ft. 6ins.(bp) x22ft.2ins. x10ft.7ins.

Lifeboats 21'6"x6'3"x2'5"

Hatch 12'0"x6'6"

Lifeboats 21'6"x6'3"x2'5"

ENGINE ROOM

BOILER ROOM

ladies saloon

Dining Saloon

horse stalls

cattle stalls

horse stalls

cattle stalls

Hatch 15'0"x7'0"

crew

2nd class accommodation

FORE HOLD 37'9"x21'0"

Hatch coaming

15'0"x6'10"x1'9"

COAL BUNKERS 9TONS

BOILER ROOM

ENGINE ROOM

COAL BUNKERS 9TONS

Ballast

Ballast

AFT HOLD 28'5"x20'0"

Hatch coaming

12'0"x6'4"x1'9"

1st class saloon

DRG No:- 09/2/98
Drawn by:- Q.Evans.

A TECHNICAL DRAWING OF THE SS ELLAN VANNIN AS COMPILED BY RON EVANS OF PONTEFRACT.

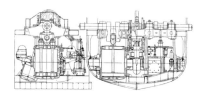

APPENDIX I

SS ELLAN VANNIN - FOR THE EXPERTS

Name	Ellan Vannin ex Monas Isle	Mona (2)	Fenella (1)	Peveril (1)	Tynwald (3)	Douglas (3) ex Dora
Hull	Iron	Iron	Iron	Steel	Steel	Steel
Built	1883	1878	1881	1884	1891	1889
Tonnage:-						
Net/Reg.	128		238	244	397	322
Gross	380	526	564	561	937	774
Under Deck	304	427	402	435	749	596
Dimensions:-						
Length o/a	207'0"	207'0"	207'0"	215'0"	276'0"	249'0"
Length b/p	198'6"	200'0"	200'0"	207'6"	265'0"	240'0"
Breadth (mld)	22'2"	26'0"	26'0"	26'0"	34'0"	30'0"
Depth (mld)	10'7"	13'3"	13'0"	13'3"	14'0"	15'2"
Draught mean	8'9"		11'4"	11'4"	11'0"	12'0"
Displ. mean			1152tons	1194tons	1600tons	1287tons
Coefficient u/d	0.652	0.62	0.595	0.62	0.594	0.545
Block coefficient			0.684	0.684	0.565	0.521
Machinery:-						
Engines	Compound	Compound	Compound	Compound	Triple Exp.	Triple Exp.
Cylinders	4/18", 34"-24"	2/33", 60"-36"	4/23", 42"-24"	4/24", 44"-24"	6/22", 36", 57"-36"	3/27",40", 65"-36"
NHP	100(RHP)	160	144	158	585	253
IHP	500		1200	1200	3800	2000
Boilers	2/10.0x9.6 single ended		2/18.0x16.1 double ended		2/18.0x16.1 double ended	
Boiler pressure	80psi		85psi	85psi	160psi	160psi
Furnaces	4nr (2'9" dia.)		6nr	6nr	16nr	12nr
Fire-grate area	55sq.ft.		131.8sq.ft.	132sq.ft.	351sq.ft.	216sq.ft.
Heating surface	2004sq.ft.		3349sq.ft.	3349sq.ft.	11,393sq.ft.	5680sq.ft.
Coal consumed	9tons/24hrs.		30tons/24hrs.	30tons/24hrs.	90tons/24hrs	42tons/24hrs.
Bunkers	18tons		65tons	65tons	120tons	52tons
Propulsion	Twin Screw	Single Screw	Twin Screw	Twin Screw	Twin Screw	Single Screw
Propeller (dia.)	7ft.3ins.		7ft.10ins.	8ft.5ins.	10ft.6ins.	11ft.9ins.
(pitch)	13ft.9ins.		13ft.6ins.	14ft.0ins.	17ft.6ins.	19ft.3ins.
(area)	17sq.ft.		22sq.ft.	24sq.ft.	41.2sq.ft.	56sq.ft.
Speed in service	12kts.	13kts.	13.5kts.	13.5kts.	18kts.	14.5kts.
Other details:-						
Hatches:- For. Aft.	15'0"x7'0" 12'0"x6'6"		8'0"x6'0" 5'0"x7'0"	8'0"x6'0" 5'0"x7'0"	7'6"x7'6" 7'6"x7'6"	6'0"x6'0" 6'0"x8'0" 5'6"x8'0"
Lifeboats:-	2nr. Lifeboats 21.6x6.3x2.5 21.6x6.3x2.5	4nr. Lifeboats 19.9x5.7x2.5 19.9x5.7x2.5 21.6x6.3x2.5 21.6x6.3x2.5	4nr. Lifeboats 19.9x5.7x2.3 19.9x5.7x2.2 21.3x6.9x2.2 21.6x6.3x2.5	4nr. Lifeboats 19.9x5.7x2.3 19.9x5.7x2.3 21.3x6.9x2.2 21.6x6.3x2.5	4nr. Lifeboats 24.6x6.8x3.1 2nr. Cutters 20.5x5.0x2.6 20.5x6.1x2.5	4nr. Lifeboats 24.3x6.8x2.8 24.3x7.0x2.7 24.8x6.0x2.4 22.4x5.5x2.4
Masts:- For. Main	60ft.0ins. 68ft.0ins.	56ft.0ins. 60ft.0ins.	47ft.3ins. 50ft.6ins.	47ft.3ins. 50ft.6ins	72ft.0ins. 72ft.0ins.	72ft.0ins. 67ft.0ins.
Passengers	299		504	504	904	506
Crew	14		28	30	50	33
Disposal	Sank, Mersey 03.12.1909	Sank, Mersey 05.08.1883	Broken up 1929	Sank Douglas 16.09.1899	Sold 1933	Sank, Mersey 16.08.1923

Block Coefficient of Finess = displacement (tons) x 35 cubic feet, divided by:- [length (**bp**) x breadth (**mld**) x draught].
Coefficient of Under Deck Tonnage = under-deck tonnage (1 ton =100cu.ft.) divided by registered dimensions.

HISTORIC SHIPS of the STEAM PACKET Co.

A COMPARATIVE TABLE OF HISTORIC SHIPS OF THE STEAM PACKET COMPANY AS COMPILED BY RON EVANS OF PONTEFRACT.

APPENDIX II
BOARD OF TRADE ENQUIRY - FULL TEXT

(No. 7338.)

"ELLAN VANNIN" (S.S.).

The Merchant Shipping Act, 1894.

In the matter of a Formal Investigation held at Liverpool on the 8th, 9th, 10th, and 12th days of March, 1910, before T. SHEPHERD LITTLE, Esquire, Stipendiary Magistrate, assisted by Vice-Admiral ARBUTHNOT, Captain OWEN R. MITCHELL, and Captain HENRY E. BATT, into the circumstances attending the loss of the British steamship "ELLAN VANNIN", with the whole of her passengers and crew, near Q1 buoy, at the entrance of the River Mersey, on the morning of the 3rd December, 1909, whilst on a voyage from Ramsey to Liverpool.

Report of Court.

The Court having carefully inquired into the circumstances attending the above-mentioned shipping casualty, finds for the reasons stated in the Annex hereto, that it is impossible to express a decided opinion as to the cause of the loss of the "Ellan Vannin", but after carefully considering all the theories which have been suggested by various witnesses and weighing them in the light of the evidence produced, the Court is of opinion that the following appears the most probable explanation of what occurred:—

The vessel passed the Bar Lightship at about 6.45 a.m. on 3rd December, the weather at the time being very bad; the wind was of hurricane force, the sea of a height of about 24 feet, and generally the weather the worst ever experienced in that vicinity. The wind and sea were slightly on the starboard quarter. Before reaching Q1 buoy she broached to and was probably swept by heavy seas which washed away the after companion, filling the after part of the vessel and causing her to sink by the stern leaving the bows out of the water. While in this position the heavy seas striking the fore part of the ship would account for the bows being broken off as described by the divers.

The Court does not consider there is any evidence of the ship having been previously in collision either with another vessel or with floating wreckage, nor do they consider that the fact of the bows breaking off under such exceptional circumstances implies structural weakness. The catastrophe by which the vessel was overtaken must have been so sudden, that there was probably no time for those on board even to put on life belts or to take any other steps to save life, which accounts for the unfortunate loss of all on board.

Dated this 12th day of March, 1910.

T. SHEPHERD LITTLE,
Judge.

We concur in the above Report.

CHARLES R. ARBUTHNOT, }
H. E. BATT, } Assessors.

Annex to the Report.

This was an Inquiry into the causes of the loss of the British steamship "Ellan Vannin" when in the vicinity of Q1 buoy in the Mersey estuary on the morning of the 3rd December, 1909, and of the loss of lives attendant thereon. It was held in the Magistrates' Room, Dale Street, Liverpool, on the 8th, 9th, 10th and 12th days of March, 1910, when Mr. Paxton represented the Board of Trade, and Mr. A. Bateson, of Counsel instructed by Messrs. Bateson, Warr & Wimshurst, appeared for the owners.

The "Ellan Vannin," formerly named the "Mona's Isle," Official Number 27260, was built as an iron paddle steamship in the year 1860, by Messrs. Tod & McGregor, of Glasgow, and was registered at the port of Douglas, Isle of Man. She was owned by the Isle of Man Steam Packet Company, Limited, Mr. William Matthias Corkhill, of Imperial Buildings, Douglas, Isle of Man, being designated in the transcript of registry as the person to whom the management of the vessel was entrusted by and on behalf of the owners by advice received 4th September, 1908, under the

seal of the Isle of Man Steam Packet Company, Limited.

She was of the following dimensions :- Length 198.6 feet, breadth 22.2 feet, and depth in hold from tonnage deck to ceiling at 'midships 10.7 feet. Her gross tonnage as amended was 379.53 tons and her registered tonnage 128.30 tons.

In the year 1883, the "Ellan Vannin" was converted from a paddle into a twin screw steamship by Messrs. Westray, Copeland & Company, of Barrow, and was fitted with two new pairs of twin screw inverted compound surface condensing engines and boilers of 100 nominal horse power with a speed of 13 knots, the diameter of the four cylinders being 18 and 34 inches respectively with a stroke of 24 inches.

The "Ellan Vannin" was a schooner rigged, two masted single bottomed, one deck vessel. She had four iron bulkheads, two water ballast tanks, one at each end of the vessel, having a total capacity of 44 tons. She had a raised quarter deck, with a house on the after part, a bridge amidships with a wheelhouse thereon from where she was steered by hand, as she had not a steam steering gear. She had a top-gallant forecastle under which was the steerage. Forward of the steerage was the forecastle, and under the forecastle, the chain locker, and abaft the chain locker, the water ballast tank. Between these compartments and the forehold there was an iron bulkhead. She had two cargo holds. The fore hatchway measured 15 feet by 6 feet 10 inches, the height of the coamings 15 inches; the after hatchway measured 12 feet by 6 feet 4 inches with coamings 15 inches.

The height of the engine room skylight above the bridge deck was 3 feet 2 inches, and from the main deck to bridge deck 7 feet 4 inches, the length being 9 feet. Her bulwarks were 4 feet 6 inches in height, with two freeing ports, one on each side, measuring 14 inches by 9 inches, and two others, one on each side, measuring 24 inches by 24 inches, and she had three deck hand pumps in connection with the bilges. She carried two lifeboats under their own davits with the necessary equipments. They rested in chocks on the bridge amidships and, judging from a photograph produced, it was very easy to get them out. The aggregate capacity of these boats was 382 cubic feet, and they were capable of accommodating 38 persons. There were also on board 320 life belts and six life buoys. These were placed in various parts of the vessel to be handy when required. She was certificated to carry 134 first-class and 165 third-class passengers and 14 of a crew, making 313 all told. She was employed in the trade between the Isle of Man and Liverpool. She was not classed, but according to the evidence, the vessel appears to have been well found and equipped in every respect.

It may be here noted that the original plans and specifications were not produced, and it would seem that they have long since ceased to exist.

According to the evidence, the vessel when laying at Douglas, Isle of Man, took the ground at low water, and while in this position her bottom as far as possible was periodically cleaned and painted.

The "Ellan Vannin" left Ramsey on the 3rd December, 1909, about 1 a.m., under the command of Mr. James Teare, who held a certificate, No. 103947. Her crew consisted of 21 hands, including the master, and she had 14 passengers. As cargo she carried about 60 tons of oats, turnips, &c., all stowed under hatches, and in addition to this, on the deck, she had some luggage and parcels and 88 sheep and one pig. The sheep and pig were secured in pens on the main deck. On leaving Ramsey she was upright and her draft was 10 feet aft and 7 feet 6 inches forward, and her freeboard was 2 feet 9 inches, the freeboard assigned by the Board of Trade being 1 foot 10 inches. As she left Ramsey the weather is described as dirty with sleet falling, and only a moderate wind, the barometer standing at 28·30. There was no suggestion made by the captain that the weather was unfit for the vessel to leave. It appears from the evidence given by those on board the lightship and other vessels that a heavy gale sprang up about 4 a.m. when the wind force was 11 and the direction N.W., with frequent rain squalls and the sea very rough. This state of things continued until 8 a.m. The sea, however, would become more dangerous as the ebb tide made strong. Shortly after 6.30 a.m. on the 3rd December an inward bound steamer passed the Bar Lightship about half a mile to the northward; her lights were seen for about five minutes, when they were obscured by a heavy shower. Taking into consideration the time usually taken by the "Ellan Vannin" from Ramsey to that point and the direction in which the steamer was approaching the bar, it is highly probably that the lights seen were those of the "Ellan Vannin". About 6.45 a.m. one of the seamen on the Bar Lightship saw what he has described as a flash lasting about one second and in the vicinity of the Bar. No other flash was seen, although the seaman and the master of the lightship watched for about 20 minutes. About 10 minutes elapsed between the sighting of the lights of the said steamer and the flash.

At 11.30 a.m. on the 3rd December, a report was received by the Mersey Docks and Harbour Board officials that Q1 black buoy was adrift. The Board's tender "Vigilant" went out to recover the buoy, and when off the Rock Lighthouse about 1.30 p.m. a lot of wreckage was seen and several dozen life belts. Part of this wreckage, including a package of mails, was recovered by the tender. The buoy was also located and on the following day was recovered. At 3.30 a.m. on the 4th December, life belts marked "Ellan Vannin", wreckage and dead sheep were found by the coastguards at Blundellsands, and later the ship's clock attached to some panelling was found. The clock had stopped at 6.50 and was not run down.

The wreck of the "Ellan Vannin" was located on the 4th December, 1,170 yards from the Bar Lightship, and 1,000 yards from the position of Q1 black buoy on a direct line between them, and broadside on to the tide. On examination by divers three bodies were found on the wreck, viz., J. C. Taubman, fireman, Edward Burke, cook, and E. Allen, a passenger. The body of Edward Burke had only underclothing on, and was found in the saloon. Up to the 16th February, fourteen other bodies were found at various points on the neighbouring coast. The names of the crew and passengers, and the list of bodies recovered are as follows:—

	Name.	Rating.	Where and when body found.
1.	James Teare ...	Master ...	Birkdale, Jan. 16, 1910.
2.	John Craine ...	Mate ...	Southport, Jan. 17, 1910.
3.	John Thos. Kinley	2nd Mate ...	—
4.	James Shepherd Cunningham	Carpenter ...	Southport, Jan. 15, 1910.
5.	John Cook ...	A.B ...	Blackpool, Feb. 16, 1910.
6.	John Benson ...	Do. ...	Ainsdale, Jan. 20, 1910.
7.	Thos. Corkish ...	Do. ...	Altcar, Jan. 19, 1910.
8.	William Kelly ...	Do. ...	—
9.	James Lambert Crawley	Do. ...	—
10.	Richard Alfred Clague	Do. ...	Birkdale, Jan. 24, 1910.
11.	Edward Bellis ...	Chief Engineer	—
12.	Fred Craine ...	2nd Engineer	—
13.	Servetus Ridings	Donkeyman ...	Formby, Jan. 10, 1910.
14.	Wm. Shimmin ...	Greaser ...	—
15.	Walter Cannell ...	Fireman ...	Waterloo, Jan. 31, 1910.
16.	John Clague Taubman	Do. ...	From Wreck, Dec. 13, 1909.
17.	Joseph Crellin ...	Do. ...	—
18.	Thomas Stubbs ...	Chief Steward	Wallasey, Jan. 29, 1910.
19.	Herbert Holland	2nd Steward ...	—
20.	Edward Burke ...	Cook ...	From Wreck, Dec. 9 1909.
21.	Eliza Collister ...	Stewardess ...	—
22.	Mark H. Joughin	Passenger ...	—
23.	W. E. Higginbotham	Do. ...	—
24.	Heaton Johnson	Do. ...	—
25.	Mrs Johnson ...	Do. ...	—
26.	D. Newall ...	Do. ...	Formby, Jan. 13, 1910.
27.	W. Williams ...	Do. ...	—
28.	Mrs W. Crix ...	Do. ...	—
29.	Mrs Crix's child ...	Do. ...	—
30.	Miss Fisher ...	Do. ...	—
31.	E. J. Blevin ...	Do. ...	Formby, Jan. 13, 1910.
32.	Thos. Quayle ...	Do. ...	Southport, Jan.13, 1910.
33.	Mrs Allen ...	Do. ...	—
34.	Ernest Allen ...	Do. ...	From Wreck, Dec. 9, 1909.
35.	Miss L. Findlay ...	Do. ...	Birkdale, Jan. 17, 1910.

Four divers were employed from time to time in examining the wreck, the first descent being made on the morning of the 5th December. Generally the condition of the wreck as reported by the divers was as follows:—

The wreck was heading about W. by S.; the fore end was broken off about 35 feet from the stem and was separated from the after part by a space estimated at about 6 feet. The after portion was nearly upright, the forward portion had a list to port of from 15° to 20° on the first examination. This list had increased to about 45° to 50° on the 12th December when the last examination was made. The break, the whole way round from rail to rail, was a straight one mainly in the line of the rivets varying not more than 6 or 8 inches either way, except on the port side where the Stringer waterway and sheer strake was attached to the forward part, and projects aft about 4 feet. The keel of the fore part at the fracture was bent up about 3 inches in 18 inches. The deck in the wake of the fracture was torn across except where the butts come; there the butts were torn out taking the deck bolts with the planks. Two divers reported an indentation of a part of the two plates below the sheer strake on the port side at the fracture, of about 18 inches in length in a vertical direction, the broken edges of the plates being bent inwards from 3 to 6 inches. One of the other divers did not notice any such indentation, and the fourth denied that it existed, but stated that some of the plates in the neighbourhood of the bilge were bent slightly inwards and upwards. The Court, however, does not attach much importance to the evidence on these points. The davits on the starboard lifeboat were stated to have been swung and guyed out. The boat was gone from the chocks. This boat was found the day after the wreck on the beach at New Brighton bottom up, cover on and all her gear in. The davits of the port lifeboat were swung out but not guyed, the boat was gone, and no trace of her has been found. The divers found the square house (which contained the saloon entrance and smoke room) on the after deck was completely washed away, only the whaling pieces on the deck being left to indicate where the house had been.

Here it may be mentioned that a theory was advanced that the "Ellan Vannin" fouled the Q1 buoy which was reported by the master of the s.s. "Heroic" to have been in place when he passed it about 6 a.m., and which was missed from its position by those on board the Bar Light vessel at 10 a.m. of the 3rd December. This buoy was recovered the following day, but no marks were found on it, and the light was still burning. Therefore the Court is unable to accept this theory, nor from a careful consideration of all the facts in evidence can it conclude that the "Ellan Vannin" was in collision either with another vessel or with any wreckage whatever. The twin screw steamship "Heroic" made the passage from Belfast to Liverpool on the night of the 2nd and the morning of the 3rd January, passing the Bar Lightship just before 6 a.m. The master, Mr. Arthur Porter, reports that the weather he experienced when approaching the mouth of the Mersey was of most exceptional violence, and that during his experience of 11 years he had never known it so bad. The wind was N.W. blowing with hurricane force, the sea broken and most dangerous particularly between the Bar Lightship and Q2 buoy. The tide was half ebb. He was doubtful of being able to pick up Q1 buoy, and had he not done so, he intended rounding to and waiting for daylight. As he sighted the buoy when off the Bar Lightship he proceeded up the channel. He further stated that his ship was pooped by heavy seas three times between the Bar Lightship and Formby Light. The ship steered badly owing to the high following seas, and with the wind on the quarter she was inclined to broach to. The ship charged from side to side and took the whole of the channel. If she had broached to she would have shipped a lot of water and he must have stopped. The "Heroic" is a much larger and more powerful ship than the "Ellan Vannin" was; she had a full poop, bridge and forecastle, and would therefore not be affected so much by the wind and sea when running before it as the "Ellan Vannin" would be.

The fact that the "Ellan Vannin" when examined was found to be partly across the channel and nearly at right angles to the wind and sea at the time she foundered indicate that she broached to before sinking. No life belts being found on any of the bodies recovered, and no distress signals having been shown (except the one which is supposed to have been seen from the Bar Lightship), points to the extreme suddenness of the disaster, probably leaving no opportunity for those on board to avail themselves of the means provided for saving life. In the opinion of several witnesses the state of the sea was such, that even had signals of distress been seen, no assistance could have been rendered.

This ship appears to have been kept in good repair and condition. She was periodically surveyed by the Board of Trade Surveyor, who gave evidence, and who had certified to her having been in a good and seaworthy condition in September last, when she showed no signs of weakness. In that month the Board of Trade certificate was renewed for one year. Plates had been removed from time to time, and these were said to have been in good condition. A plan has been put in, showing the results of drilling a large number of plates in various sections of the vessel in 1902, and from this it appears that up to that date there had been no appreciable wasting of the iron. The fact, however, cannot be ignored that this vessel was 50 years old, and it is possible that some corrosion may have occurred at places that were difficult of access (for example, the chain locker), and this may possibly have led to her breaking at this particular place, although there was nothing to indicate that such was the case. The chain locker was about 26 feet long, and had a wooden platform on which to slow the chain. It is well known that if corrosion takes place at all, this is the most likely part for it to do so.

Although no importance is attached to it, the fact may be mentioned that a small bottle was produced which had been picked up on the 17th January on the beach near the Altcar Rifle Range, which contained a slip of paper purporting to be a message written by E. Burke, the cook of the "Ellan Vannin", stating that the ship had been in collision with an unknown vessel and was sinking. The appearance of this bottle was not consistent with its having been exposed for such a long period, the paper label being intact and still adhering stiffly to the glass. The message was in a different handwriting from the signature and was quite dissimilar to the writing of the cook. The signature E. Burke was a poor imitation of three signatures of E. Burke which were put in, and the Court is clearly of opinion that the writing contained in the bottle was spurious.

In coming to a conclusion as to the way in which the vessel probably foundered and her fore end broken off, the Court placed much reliance on the evidence of Lieutenant Mace, the Marine Surveyor of the Mersey Docks and Harbour Board, that he had on several occasions known ships to go down by the stern leaving their bows projecting above the water and so remaining for a considerable period.

At the conclusion of the evidence, Mr. Paxton for the Board of Trade submitted the following questions for the opinion of the Court:—

(1) What was the cost of the vessel to her owners? What was her value at the time she sailed from Ramsey on her last voyage? What insurances were effected upon and in connection with her?

(2) When the vessel left Ramsey on or about the 3rd December last—
   (a)   Was she in good and seaworthy condition as regards hull and equipments?
   (b)   Was her cargo properly stowed and secured from shifting, and was the weight so distributed as to make the vessel easy in a seaway?
   (c)   Had she the required freeboard and was she in good trim for a voyage to Liverpool?

(3) What was the cause of the loss of the "Ellan Vannin" and the loss of life?

Mr. A. Bateson having addressed the Court on behalf of the owners of the "Ellan Vannin", the Court gave judgement as above, and returned the following answers to the questions of the Board of Trade:—

(1) The original cost of the "Ellan Vannin" to her owners in 1860 when she was built was £10,673. She was originally a paddle steamer. In 1883 she was converted into a twin screw steamer, and at the same time had an overhaul at Barrow. The cost of conversion and of the overhaul was given as nearly £9,000. In 1891 she had a thorough overhaul by the Naval Armament and Construction Company, at Barrow, at a cost of £2,914. In 1900, after a collision, repairs were executed by A. & J. Inglis, of Partick, Glasgow, at a cost of about £800. General repairs were executed by the owners from time to time up to 1909, including a new main deck, the cost of which was roughly estimated to be £5,000. The cost of the

ship to the owners was, therefore, about £28,387.

Her declared value when she sailed from Ramsey on her last voyage was £5,000. She was insured for £5,000, the owners taking one seventh (£714), leaving as a risk to the underwriters £4,286.

(2) (a) She was in good and seaworthy condition as regards hull and equipments when she left Ramsey on or about the 3rd December last.

(b) Her cargo was properly stowed and secured from shifting and the weight so distributed as to make the vessel easy in a seaway.

(c) She had the required freeboard and was in good trim for a voyage to Liverpool.

(3) In the absence of any direct evidence as to the circumstances under which the vessel foundered, it is impossible for the Court to express a decided opinion as to the cause of the loss of the "Ellan Vannin", but after carefully considering all the theories which have been suggested by various witnesses and weighing them in the light of the evidence produced, the Court is of opinion that the following appears the most probable explanation of what occurred:—

The vessel passed the Bar Lightship at about 6.45 a.m. on the 3rd December, the weather at the time being very bad; the wind was of hurricane force, the sea of a height of about 24 feet, and generally the weather the worst ever experienced in that vicinity. The wind and sea were slightly on the starboard quarter. Before reaching Q1 buoy she broached to and was probably swept by heavy seas which washed away the after companion, filling the after part of the vessel and causing her to sink by the stern, leaving the bows out of the water. While in this position the heavy seas striking the forepart of the ship would account for the bows being broken off as described by the divers.

The Court does not consider there is any evidence of the ship having been previously in collision either with another vessel or with floating wreckage, nor does it consider that the fact of the bows breaking off under such exceptional circumstances implies structural weakness. The catastrophe by which the vessel was overtaken must have been so sudden that there was probably no time for those on board even to put on life belts or to take any other steps to save life, which accounts for the unfortunate loss of all on board.

T. SHEPHERD LITTLE,
Judge.

We concur in the above Report.

CHARLES R. ARBUTHNOT, }
H. E. BATT, } Assessors.

I concur with the above except as regards the answer to question 3. My theory to that answer is as follows:—

On the morning of the 3rd December last, the vessel when in the vicinity of Q1 buoy broached to or had to be brought to against a heavy sea running on her starboard side, which caused for some unknown reason the butt straps under the chain locker to suddenly give way, when a strong inrush of water would occur filling the fore compartment, and finally the whole of the butt straps on the ship's side giving way, causing the vessel to go down head first with little or no warning, which points to her being found by the divers completely broken in two from under the chain locker upwards.

The vessel on changing her course would bring the full force of wind on her starboard side and may possibly with her port bow have touched or collided with Q1 buoy, causing the buoy to break adrift on the morning of the 3rd December last.

OWEN R. MITCHELL,
Assessor.

Liverpool, 14th March, 1910.

(*Issued in London by the Board of Trade on the 8th day of April, 1910.*)

INDEX

INDEX

INDEX